VHS ATE MY BRAIN

By Andrew Hawnt

©Andrew Hawnt 2014

VHS ATE MY BRAIN

By Andrew Hawnt
©Andrew Hawnt 2014

The right of Andrew Hawnt to be identified as the author of this work has been asserted by him in accordance with the Designs, Copyrights and Patents act of 1988.

All rights reserved.

Please don't pirate or copy this book, as I'm broke and need the money. Plus, legal action is tedious and I'd rather watch a film. Preferably on VHS, as long as my tracking doesn't screw me about.

Released and promoted through DREAMRIDER MEDIA

www.andrewhawnt.com

For my son, Alexander.

*This is about those funny black plastic things
your daddy has so many of.*

And

*For the members of HORROR VHS COLLECTORS UNITE!
You freak me out. But you're still awesome.*

Hmm... what to watch tonight?

INTRODUCTION

Hello. You may not know me, but we'll soon sort that out. I'm Andrew. I like horror films and caffeine. I collect obscure horror flicks on VHS. Yes, I said VHS, that dead format which seems so obsolete now, and yet once defined a cinematic generation. Possibly even two generations. I'm not alone in this, as a cursory look online will quickly tell you. I am one of a growing number of VHS Collectors around the world, and we all have a tale to tell regarding how we discovered the format, the films it brought us, and what those tapes, films and times meant to us in the evolution of our lives.

This is not intended as a history of the medium, as there are scholars far more knowledgeable than myself out there who are able to give you the full story of those magical plastic boxes of tape. This is intended to be a love letter to a format which had a massive amount of potential and fulfilled it in grand style. While VHS brought home video to a global market (sorry Betamax, I loved you too, but VHS took that accolade quite spectacularly), it also brought a universe of bizarre and wonderful entertainment to millions of people like me.

Told with honesty and a deep and abiding love for genuinely bad films the format blessed me with, I hope you can find some of the magic of VHS in these pages, and find out about a little of the mindset which VHS horror collectors like myself (and possibly you too, considering you were kind enough to pick up this book) are afflicted with.

So sit down, adjust the tracking a bit, wait for the copyright warning to pass, then Simon Mayo telling you 'THE

VIDEO YOU HAVE RENTED IS CLASSIFIED AS AN 18, MEANING THERE COULD BE SCENES OF VIOLENCE, EXPLODING HEADS, INTESTINES BEING CHEWED AND SWEAR WORDS WORSE THAN "BOLLOCKS" (or whatever that bloody warning said) and then the tantalizing moments of darkness before we begin. I hope you enjoy this feature presentation.

RENTING DREAMS FOR PENNIES

If you are of a certain age, then you will be able to remember the joys and the horrors of the video rental shop very clearly. If you don't remember those magical places, then I do feel you missed out on, well, many hours of frustration and indecision, mainly. Going to the video shop is a ritual that is now long gone, and that makes me feel very old indeed as I did it far too often and have ever been able to fill that void in my life, which probably explains why I am so very neurotic and fidgety now. Or that could be the caffeine addiction, fatherhood or a constant war against temptation when there are chicken wings in the freezer. I miss video shops very much, as they evoke a time of life when I still had some hope left, some hair left, and some disposable income left.

The humble VHS tape was (and still is, for some of us) a very important part of life, stretching beyond video rental shops and into our homes, allowing us to record and re-watch anything we wanted, until the tape wore out or we got so sick of messing about with the tracking that we kicked the machine to death.

It was rental shops which grabbed my imagination first though, and we shall begin by revisiting what made video shops so special. A lot of the shops and the videos are gone, replaced by DVDs, Blu Rays, streaming media and more. The chains will soon be gone too completely too, especially following the final downfall of Blockbuster. Companies are facing ever more competition from online streaming services and outlets online where you can buy DVDs and suchlike brand new for the equivalent, or less, than renting them.

The world has moved on from the video age, and the feel of the independent video shop is long gone, and is much missed. There was one video shop in particular that I spent a great deal of time in during my teenage years and my twenties, and that shop, although now closed and gone, lives on in my memory as a place that I felt welcome. As a comics/horror/rock geek with an awkward, nerdy air about me, there weren't many places I could say that about at the time.

The video shop at the bottom of the hill served me very well indeed for several years, and opened my mind not only to a universe of weird entertainment, but also helped to shape the oddball that I would become, inspiring me and giving me something that I felt a part of. Getting a video and some snacks is a ritual that millions of people all over the world would carry out on a regular basis, often making what could be a very solitary hobby into a very social event.

Enjoyed alone or with company, videos could take you anywhere you wanted to go, as long as your machine would play the damn tapes and the people who had rented them before you had A: rewound them and B: not taped *Eastenders* over them by accident. The practice of renting videos even had its own internal hierarchy; overnight for new releases, two days for lesser releases, and up to a week for older titles (that was the practice at a number of stores I frequented anyway). Then there were all the special offers and the little deals you could strike with the proprietors.

I shall tell you the story of visiting an average video shop to sum up the delights and the heartbreaks of that particular piece of pop culture history. I shall do so by immortalizing that much-missed video shop at the bottom of the hill, the place I spent so many hours trying to decide what to rent: Metro Video in Malin Bridge, Sheffield.

METRO VIDEO: It's all your fault!

Metro Video, oh how I miss you. Nestled between a greasy old cafe and, hmm, it was either a hairdressers or a paintball place (possibly both were there for a while), the shop with the long blue sign with yellow lettering and windows full of cardboard video adverts was the most magical place in the world for me for a good long while. That shop took a great deal of money from me over the years, but it was worth every damn penny.

The shop took up two floors, incorporating two rooms downstairs and one long room upstairs. As you walked into the shop, the whole room to your right was taken up with new releases; row upon row of brand new tapes staring back at you and luring you closer with lurid promises of action, danger, suspense, gore, laughter and/or titillation. At the end of that room lay the counter, with snacks available either side of it, a drinks fridge and a formidable wall of thousands of tapes behind it.

At one side of the counter there as also a box of used video posters, which the owners of the place would either sell for 10p or hand out for free (it varied). Plus, if you wanted the adverts that were currently up on the walls (all beautifully arranged in elaborate displays), be they posters, cardboard standees or other cutouts, all you had to do was ask the staff and your name would be put onto the back of what you want, and it would be put aside for you once the item had fulfilled its advertising purposes.

I got so many movie posters, sample video sleeves and stuff from that place it was unreal. The place was run by absolutely lovely people, and their prices were very reasonable indeed. However, even though their prices were great, it was something of an event for me to rent a full-price new release. The magic for me lay around the corner, in the more mid-range releases, which were cheaper, and often more insane than the big name titles.

Those films were my gateway into the world of cult and low-budget movies, mainly of a horror or science fiction nature, which further served to shape the jaded, bitter geek I am now. Ah, but the real magic was upstairs, in the windowless cavern where old films went to die, or at least to be offered at two tapes for a quid overnight. It's from that silent room, stacked floor to ceiling with racks of beautifully arranged VHS boxes, that I took home more tapes than any one person should really ever sit through.

I systematically rented out pretty much every single tape in the horror and sci-fi sections upstairs in that room of dreams, as well as making a big dent in the action and comedy sections. The age of a film didn't matter to me. I just wanted to see them, to experience them in the setting I enjoyed the most – in my room, with snacks and the numbers on my old digital clock creeping deeper and deeper into the small hours of the next morning.

Why, I hear you cry in dismay, didn't I go out and meet people? Why didn't I get a life rather than sitting alone watching endless horror movies and rewinding them to watch the trailers? Why didn't I do something more useful with my time? Uh... like what? Watch football? Go out and get mashed every night in crap indie bars like everyone else I knew at the time? No thanks. I had my films. I had my routine. I needed to escape from a world I have never, ever felt much of a part of, and the only way I could do that with any level of success was to rent a stack of cheap films from Metro Video at the bottom of the hill, close the curtains and press PLAY.

How can I be nostalgic about years spent sat in front of a TV? Because I loved it. Every second of it. Those films took me away from what was going on outside the house, which wasn't pretty in those days, thanks to local gangs and a lot of trouble on our street. I felt imprisoned in the house a bit, and those films gave me a gateway to other countries, other worlds, other times, and countless adventures.

But enough about rose-tinted nostalgia. I revisited Metro Video a few times before it finally closed down, long after I had moved to another city as adult life took hold and started to wring a lot of the joy out of my existence with bills and having to be sensible and grown-up. Revisiting the place was weird, as in its last years of existence the focus had, of course, shifted from VHS tapes and onto DVDs and new generation video games. The upstairs room vanished, blocked off behind a door and hidden by posters and standees. A basket of old VHS tapes sat by the door, tempting me with its wares. Each time I went back in, I would pick up a couple of tapes from the basket which would make my geeky heart leap with joy. There I was, at long last, able to purchase some of the tapes I had fetishised years earlier, and for a pittance. Those tapes take pride of place in my collection to this day.

Of course, the visits back there became ever more infrequent, and I kept telling myself I should go and get a photo of the place, just in case I ever wrote a book about my love for VHS (oh, wait... oops), but then, one day recently, I went back there to do just that and found the place had gone. Seeing something else in the space Metro Video had always been for as long I could remember was strange. Jarring. Another piece of my younger days was gone, vanished into memory, and probably not remembered all that well by very many people around there, despite their years of service.

So, with that in mind, I'd like to thank Metro Video for giving me so much happiness, for renting me horror and sci-fi which would make my dreams so much bigger, for selling me new releases cheap now and again as they liked me, for saving me posters and for, well, existing at all. Your shop lives on again in these words, such as they are, and such as I am.

THE PERFECT VHS NIGHT IN

During the height of my VHS rental days in my late teens, I developed THE PERFECT VHS NIGHT IN, a routine which has stuck with me to this day when I get the rare opportunity to have a film night. Of course, circumstances, my hairline, my home situation and indeed the formats have changed since those heady/turbulent/frustrating days (although VHS will always be my one true film love), but the ritual remains largely the same.

In the original incarnation of the PERFECT VHS NIGHT IN, first of all I would go to Metro Video and pick up at least three films. One would generally be a mid-list new-ish film which had recently come down from full price to the next layer of cheapness down. The other two films would always be from the magical wonderland of the Upstairs Room, where the films were two for 1.00 to rent. Of the three films chosen, there would be three combinations I would always stick with.

The first would be the variety selection – one horror, one sci-fi and one comedy. The second would be one horror, one action and one comedy. The third would be two horror movies and one 'Film I Should Have Seen By Now'. The first version of this stack would generally be the one I'd go for the most. Hell, when I did go for the third option I'd rarely get to the last film and instead just replay the trailers on the first two. Trailers were far more interesting than broadening my horizons.

With the films chosen, my attention would turn to the accompaniment required. Drinks and snacks would have to be procured, and they had to be specific things. There would have to be a large single pack of crisps (potato chips to my US friends) and at least two litres of carbonated soft drinks (IRN BRU was a favourite). The stash was completed by a very specific kind of popcorn from the Morrison's supermarket chain.

    They used to do giant bags of absolutely vile and luridly coloured popcorn for about a quid, and the one I needed for a night of VHS mayhem was the luminous hot pink variety. It tasted of nothing but sugar and chemicals, any semblance of a flavour done away with in favour of what can only be described as diabetes waiting to happen. Here in my 30s I couldn't hope to have a similar night of sugar-laden action lest my heart explode and my fragile, movie-warped brain dribble out of my nose.

    The ritual continued. The films couldn't begin until a good hour. Usually around 10pm. I was a teenager with a somewhat flexible college schedule and as such could pretty much stay up until I dropped, which I often did. Once the sitcoms had ended for the evening had ended, I would gather the troops (i.e. my supplies) and arrange the perfect nest in my room. This involved pillows and the duvet from my bed plus extra cushions. A notebook and pen would be beside the pile of comfort, in case inspiration struck during the films (I had pretensions of being a writer someday. Look how far that got me. I needn't have bothered...), along with any recent comic and magazine purchases (for during the dull bits with dialogue, between fight scenes or shots of people getting their heads torn to bits). I would basically develop a siege mentality, desperate not to move unless it was for toilet breaks or to switch tapes at the end of a flick.

    And then came the main event – putting the tapes on. The trailers were often the main event for me, even with great films. It's trailers that get me excited for a movie, and when there would be a series of trailers in a row before the main feature presentation began, I was comping at the bit to see those films. Every one. Even the ones which were clearly rubbish. No matter the genre. I truly believe that the art of the film trailer is one of the greatest skills in the entertainment industry.

It is completely possible to take an absolutely awful film and make a stunning trailer out of it. We see enough evidence of that today. Some things never change. The thing is, a lot of the time back then, you would fully expect the film to be a steaming pile of crap and not the masterpiece the trailer made it out to be. Nevertheless, trailers were always massively entertaining (and thus I now have an addition to those trailer DVDs you can get hold of, plus the ubiquitous game of YouTube movie trailer tag). I would never fast-forward through them. I felt that if I didn't watch the trailers, I wasn't getting my money's worth.

And thus the night would continue with films back-to-back, usually coming to a close sometime around 4am. However, it would often end earlier on the nights where I had become a little too comfortable and conked out before the end of the first, or halfway through the second of the night.

But why would such a simple ritual become so important to me? These things sound so lame when typed up, so pointless and hum-drum, but they were important to me. It takes us back to escapism. I wanted to think about something other than the shitty and directionless state my life was in. I wanted to sink into a comfortable place and have my mind blown by violence and gore and nudity and bad jokes and cheap special effects. I wanted to be anyone but there and anyone but me. The trailers, the movies, their covers and even the blurbs on the back all helped me cope with the horrors of everyday life, which at times grew so formidable I truly felt there would be no salvation.

Well I did find salvation, and it was trapped inside plastic cases full of magnetic tape. Those nights in my room, sat in front of bad movies with snacks that would eventually fuck up my body were some of the only happy times I knew as a teenager. I like my own company when it comes to watching movies, as I don't want to wonder what anyone else is thinking. I like bad films, and having someone else there mouthing off about how shitty the latest *Warlock* or *Project Shadowchaser* film would just annoy me.

Those nights were good. There was solace in those video tapes and the sugary snacks. Solace I badly needed as an unpopular, weird-looking teenager with a reedy voice and bad hair. The voice is still odd, but the hair is long gone now. However, my love of a good night of snacks and films remains, even though the opportunity for them is a rare thing indeed of late. Here and now, the snacks have become home-made savoury fare and the drinks have become alcoholic in nature, but the ritual remains pretty much the same. Mind you, I haven't had any of the lurid pink popcorn in about fifteen years now, which is probably for the best, considering the demented dreams it gave me (see? Films don't send people insane – I blame the popcorn). I guess it's a case of finding my happy place, and where better to find a happier place than inside a good/bad/trashy movie?

Just don't you dare fast -forward through the trailers.

THE CULTURAL IMPORTANCE OF VHS

It's apparently easy for a lot of people to forget just how big the impact of VHS on the cultural landscape was. In an age of ever-changing media formats, be they of a physical nature or streaming, the focus is very much on the new and the cutting-edge. Well, to be honest that's always been the way, but few formats ever enjoyed such a lengthy lifespan as VHS tapes. Vinyl is arguably pretty much the only thing which had a similar lifespan to the magical plastic boxes that creepy guys like me are obsessed with. While the video recorders went through a huge evolutionary process as the decades wore on, the tapes themselves remained largely the same as they always were. Pretty much.

The cultural impact of VHS recorders and VHS tapes really cannot be underestimated. I mean, here was a format which was widely available and eventually very affordable, which enabled people all over the world to record and playback material that would otherwise have been lost after one broadcast. It also, of course, gave rise to the video rental industry, which opened up the eyes of the world to a universe of entertainment, information and more with which to fill their heads when it suited them, instead of having to stick to a schedule.

Everyone who used a video recorder has a selection of semi-nostalgic anecdotes about doing so, usually surrounding issues with tracking, or trying to cut the adverts out of stuff you were taping off the TV, or the size of the early machines, or the 'Video Library' cases which were supposed to look like hardback books, and so on. These things were very much part of the fabric of peoples' lives for a very long time. As an example, as a kid I would go to the video shop with my dad on a friday night and we'd spend ages trying to find a video that was suitable for everyone who was going to watch it and seemed relatively entertaining. Sadly, as I was a kid this meant I never got to rent the good stuff, i.e. badass horror movies, as everyone else was too chicken to risk watching anything with even a hint of gore in it. Looking back to those days now, I remember seeing a massive number of tapes which would go on to become cult classics, but at the time were exciting because they were taboo.

Later, once I was into my teenage years, as well as a library of movies, cartoons and TV shows in my bedroom, I was an avid recorder of sitcoms. I rapidly built up a huge stack of tapes of sitcoms, sci-fi shows, music videos, films and more, and it astounds me that I ever thought I'd watch much of it again. The thing is, even though I didn't re-watch everything I taped, I did re-watch a hell of a lot of it and enjoyed it. In fact, some of those tapes from my teenage years are now much-cherished treasures to me, as they not only contain the original broadcasts of TV that I loved, they also contain adverts, idents, news reports, interviews and a load of other stuff which would otherwise have been lost by the ravages of time. VHS tapes are essentially time capsules. We didn't know it at the time, but by taping stuff off the TV, we were preserving chunks of popular culture, and indeed moments of historical importance, without really knowing it.

My lady just reminded me of something that I must talk about – the practice of 'Filling up the tape'. This was where you'd recorded a bunch of stuff you wanted to keep, but couldn't deal with leaving any blank space at the end of tapes you'd pid out for. This gave rise to some very odd compilations erupting after the main content of a tape had come to an end. I tended to fill up remaining space on tapes with music videos, live performances of songs by bands I liked (or at least didn't mind) from magazine shows, short cartoons or even more random stuff like chunks of culture shows, interviews, movie trailers from film shows and more. Quite often, if I'd taped something live instead of setting the timer for it, I may well have fallen asleep by the end of it (I watched a hell of a lot of late-night TV and bad movies as a teenager) and just left the machine going until the tape ran out. This often filled the tape with late-night news reports, chunks of obscure Bollywood movies or niche culture shows which couldn't really be shown earlier in the day due to the fact their collective audience was made up of insomniacs and a dozen anoraks.

Of course, as this is England, this also made it very likely that I'd tape an hour of *Ceefax* or *Oracle* Teletext pages (now I'm really showing my age), or job listings with muzak over them. This was long before the days of 24-hour broadcasting (with UK channels anyway). Once we got cable (and I was lucky enough to have my own cable connection in my teenage bedroom independent of the one downstairs), the issue of filling up tapes was something that became much easier. I mean, I was suddenly inundated with trash that I wanted to lap up, crap music videos, endless channels filled with utter nonsense, random short films, foreign channels spewing out demented bikini-girls-and-gunge-and-old-guys-being-sleazy game shows, hilariously dubbed movies and more.

Actually, speaking of foreign channels, I used to tape chunks of some of those bad foreign game shows and soap operas on some tapes, cutting together really weird mixtape-style affairs which ended up looking like trippy spoofs of actual TV. The end of a video tape tells you a lot about the person who has recorded it, and like the art of the audio mixtape, a good video compilation is an art form which has now died out pretty much altogether.

But the expanse of VHS went much further than just home use. While it was intended as a home entertainment format, VHS also found its way into schools, businesses, services, governmental departments and countless other places, its influence and usefulness stretching far beyond just watching a movie. The VHS phenomenon became part of millions, perhaps billions, of lives across the planet, and its influence is still felt to this day, despite what the kids may say to the contrary.

Hell, we've had TiVo for ages with our TV package and we still say "I'm taping that" when we're going to record something to the Hard Drive in our TV box. I would imagine a lot of other people do this too. Some terms still mean the same thing, even though they don't. Erm. I know what I mean. I hope you do too.

The feeling of nostalgia towards video rental shops and taking ages to choose a tape for the night is just one part of the cultural impact of the VHS era. Its profound influence on popular culture went on to shape the rise of DVD and indeed Blu-Ray, such was the format's genius, and the echoes of VHS packaging can still be seen in the new releases of today. As analogue media began to die out, its influence on the way media is packaged and sold remains in effect, even with streaming media and downloads – they still have movie posters and cover images inspired by the VHS covers of yore.

While the format is now dead aside from collectors and a few diehard companies releasing special runs of rare films (along with the occasional relatively big release from companies, such as the films House of the Devil and V/H/S on the format), its cultural impact remains powerful and lives on in the hearts and minds of anyone who ever had to mess about with the tracking in order to watch a flick.

WHY HORROR?

What is it about horror movies that pulls people like us into the genre and doesn't let go? What is it about a genre which was created to scare and unsettle people that makes for such powerful entertainment?

Horror is something which has its origins in a very primal part of our brains, and horror entertainment taps into that primal instinct and provides us with a rush of fear and excitement. We know these films are fiction, nothing more than elaborate examples of smoke and mirrors, but we can't help but be thrilled when the very worst things happen on our screens. There is a perverse thrill in seeing carnage and bloody mayhem, and for horror fans, the messier the better.

My fascination with the horror genre began at school. I was horrendously unpopular, and escapist entertainment soon became my drug of choice as a way of dealing with the day-to-day bullying, name-calling and general misery. Comics, cartoons, sci-fi TV and so on all became my 'other' world very quickly as soon as I discovered them, but at the age of 12 I discovered horror and the power that it contained. Horror fiction had the power to freak people out just by having them seeing me read it, which ended up with me reading Stephen King's *IT* and William Peter Blatty's *The Exorcist* and a few others during that year.

Those books showed me that words could be terrifying and entertaining, but they also had a strange side effect: The perception of me seemed to shift a bit, from just an average little nerd into a little nerd who had a head full of scary things. For one English class project, we had to write a story about a journey. Any journey. While a bunch of kids wrote stories about holidays or shopping trips, I wrote a piece called *Place Of Armageddon*, in which a young boy is sucked into another dimension by dark forces, and discovers a world filled with zombies and mutants intent on butchering him and taking our realm for themselves.

    A couple of days later, my parents were called into school by the headmistress, who was freaked out by me trying to freak out the other kids. She asked me why it seemed that I didn't want to make any friends. I asked if she'd *seen* the other kids in the school. She sighed and said "Point taken." Basically, my school was full of creatures that were little more than turd-filled fleshbags with a penchant for random acts of violence and the collective IQ of a shoebox of lint.

    Horror films were seen as something of a badge of honour at the time (and a good way of sounding a bit more badass than you really were. Keep in mind this was the north of England and as such something of a war-zone as a kid. Mind you, I think that's the way for pretty much every kid in the world. School is a pain), with myself and a bunch of classmates trying to outdo each others' knowledge of films we hadn't seen, but which we wanted to make out we knew them off by heart in order to sound cool and like we had access to taboo tapes.

    I remember one example in particular – *The Burning*. I love that film now, but only finally got to see it in recent years. Back in the day, when it was still banned over here, when I was at school me and a bunch of other nerds-in-waiting would talk about our favourite scenes in the film, which we had completely invented ourselves as none of us had ever seen the thing. Funnily enough, the scenes we came up with weren't that far off the mark (see that movie – it rocks).

    Horror movies have that power. Even the thought of them is enough to instill excitement and the feeling that you're in the presence of something wrong and powerful. It's that edge of slight danger when exposing yourself to a good horror movie which draws a lot of fans into the genre in the first place. It's a rush. A buzz like no other cinematic treat can provide.

Horror is a genre which often challenges the viewer, and when done well it can be a massively satisfying thing to experience. Mind you, when it's done badly it can sometimes be just as much fun. After all, as VHS viewers we have been exposed to some truly awful films which literally only a handful of people worldwide give a crap about, and we love them. Do we have bad taste? Are we uncultured and ignorant? Nah. We are fully aware when something's good or bad, but a lot can be forgiven on VHS. The low quality resolution of VHS allows for cheap effects to look a little more seamless, and while it can't make a bad film good, it can provide the viewer with all manner of entertainments.

VHS horror is a fetish pursuit for a lot of people around the world now, and quite rightfully so. The modern horror scene, to me, is really struggling to come up with anything new with really engages with an audience, so a renewed interest in older, more unique titles is understandable. There are moments of brilliance in modern horror movies which I must recognize and respect for what they are, but for me a lot of them are lacking a certain undeniable spark and feeling of taboo and tension that horror movies of the video era held for me. Maybe I'm just getting old. Maybe I'm becoming a bit of a snob (although how it's possible to be a snob about films as bad as half of the ones I watch, I'm not entirely sure). Maybe I'm right. Maybe I'm slightly right. Maybe the films were better, the scene less controlled and more open to wild ideas. Maybe I need to get out more.

For me, I like horror movies because they're fun, they're exciting, the filmmaking and special effects processes fascinate me, and with older horror movies, they provide an interesting look at a time when the world and the movie industry were very different. So why horror? Come on, why not?

BUYING NEW RELEASES... BACK IN THE DAY

The days of seeing new releases of films and TV series on VHS tapes in individual boxes, double-packs or box sets are now long gone, but the memory of those days lives on with people like me, and when I think of seeing those alluring rows of new release tapes in Our Price and Virgin Megastores and all those other places which don't exist here any more, I am reminded of the excitement that came with each purchase.

Of course, before you bought anything there would be a great deal of time spent choosing which title to lay down your cash for. This could sometimes go on for hours, depending on what was out that week and the size of each particular shop's selection.

Choosing a VHS tape to buy is an art that is now long gone for all but a few dedicated weird types like us, and I can't help but feel nostalgic for the days when shelves upon shelves of mint condition videos were lined up before me, their tapes sealed in shrink wrap within their clamshell cases. I can see them now, in places like long-gone branches of HMV, Our Price, Virgin Megastore, Woolworths and all the others. Racks of new releases and then endless aisles of standard catalogue titles and classics, filling music/entertainment shops up to the brim with goodies to enjoy.

Buying horror movies in that era was an exciting prospect to me, as I came to the genre young and didn't get to buy the films myself for a long time. It was rare that I could get anything resembling horror from mainstream shops due to the age I was, and thus for the most part my purchases in those days were mainly things like those old *Star Trek: The Next Generation* and *Star Trek: Deep Space Nine* tapes with two episodes on apiece, or 1980s comedies, which is another genre I've always felt a special affinity for, but for different reasons to my fascination with horror movies. 80s comedies followed a certain set of production and storytelling rules which I found comforting throughout the dull

1990s and beyond. I mean, how can anyone fail to be entertained by films like *Porky's* or *Stripes* or *Adventures In Babysitting* or *Planes, Trains and Automobiles?*

Here and now, most of those shops are gone, with only HMV still holding onto the idea of being a large-scale entertainment chain. There's Fopp, but I believe they're owned by HMV now and are used primarily for offloading excess HMV stock at discount prices, or at least that's how it feels. Fopp is a brilliant store, if you have one nearby, as they carry nothing but CDs, DVDs, Blu-rays and books. There's a bit of tech and a few shirts and things, but their main focus is the films and music. Then you go to HMV itself and there's almost no music whatsoever and the film sections are dying under the weight of tedious product being put out by an industry which is thrashing around in all directions in order to try and stay afloat. That said, the local HMV has recently been redesigned and is featuring much more music and film again, so maybe there's still a little bit of hope that these places will continue to cater to an audience that is still out there which is maybe being ignored by the mass media.

So yeah, in a completely nostalgic way, I miss the old music shops and the rows of VHS tapes, the promo posters, the free t-shirts, the insert cards and giveaway leaflets inside the shrink-wrap. New VHS on a large scale may be a thing of the past, but those days and those tapes live on in the memories of people like me, and maybe people like you too. I wonder what your memories are of those days. I like to think they are similar to my own. It's good to know others understand what things like this mean to our culture, our development in the arts, and our own sense of transience.

VHS COVERS AS AN ART FORM

The VHS cover was, and indeed is, a beautiful art form in its own right. More often than not, in the golden age of genre VHS releases, the covers were a damn sight better than the films which lay behind them. It was an age prior to the legions of five-minute Photoshop jobs which have robbed cinema of one of its most powerful aesthetics, and many of those images live on long after the films they advertised have faded into even deeper obscurity than when they first came out.

Look at *Mutant Hunt* or *Metalstorm: The Destruction Of Jared-Syn* or *Eliminators*. The covers of those SF/fantasy flicks made them look vast and epic and breathtaking, whereas the reality was that they were about as cheap as it gets and something of a chore to sit through (although *Eliminators* is a lot of dumb fun, despite a weak middle act). The video sleeve is something which became akin to a star in its own right.

At the horror end of things, look at the original VHS cover for Deodato's *Cannibal Holocaust* and its ilk. Those lurid, graphic covers which featured gore and mayhem by the bucketload were a major factor in gaining those films so much notoriety. The thing is, VHS sleeves had to be this way. They had to be garish and outlandish and promise so much more than the films had to offer, as companies simply didn't have the budget to raise interest from audiences any other way.

The practice of buying up older films to rerelease saw the rise of new artwork for old content, too. That meant that behind the cheap and nasty new cover, there was an old film which bore only a tangential resemblance to whatever madness was going on in the artwork. That adds a certain value to me, as it really can't get much cheaper and more tacky than that. Love it.

VHS covers for a lot of horror films were the only advertising the distributors could afford, and as such they became an art form and one of the things I miss the most about the VHS era. I mean, come on, look at movie posters and DVD/Blu Ray covers now. They suck so much. Utterly boring. Much like a lot of modern content. At least VHS covers had some style, even if the films themselves certainly didn't!

FINDING VHS IN LESS THAN PLEASANT PLACES

There was a certain amount of excitement for me from the practice of buying second hand VHS tapes from less than reputable sources. This made up for the difficulty in getting horror movies from mainstream sources. My initiation into the ranks of underaged horror fans began around the age of 12, thanks to me being cheeky enough to try and buy cheap horror films from dodgy market stalls. There were two within close proximity to each other; One outdoors between the Castle and Sheaf markets in my hometown of Sheffield (years before the Sheaf was demolished), and one in a far scarier place – the upstairs 'speciality' shops over one side of the Castle market.

Those shops were a strange netherworld to me. They were dank and dirty, tacky and dilapidated, but teeming with charm (and probably TB as well). Along the walkway once you had braved the filth-ridden staircase outside the market's main entrance, you were greeted by the smell of piss from the path itself and the musty air of places which had been left behind by the passage of time.

One large place housed four or five small stalls selling records, stamps, books and magazines. That was an early hunting ground for cheap metal vinyl for my burgeoning rock and metal fixation, but it was a couple of doors down from there, at the video shop run by a lady with questionable morals (or who just didn't care), where my imagination really took flight.

I can't remember what the place was called, or even if it actually had a name over its door, but I do remember the racks of ex-rental video tapes at 1.99 each and their gaudy covers and titles. The first two tapes I bought from there were to build on my limited experience with genre film at the time (*A Nightmare on Elm Street 3: Dream Warriors* and *Day of the Dead* were very early titles my impressionable mind was exposed to) were the schlocky comedy-horror sequel *Return Of The Living Dead Part 2* and martial arts b-movie cheese masterpiece *China O'Brien*. Not the best films ever made, but they were magical to me.

You may pass judgement on a child being able to watch adult themed movies at such a young age, but those films were clearly fantasy (be they horror, action, sci-fi or otherwise), and light-years away from the torture porn which calls itself horror right now. The horror films I watched at that age had a sense of humour and real atmosphere, and it was very clear to me that it was all pretend. My childhood fascination with special effects may have had something to do with it, as by the time I saw horrific gore scenes, I could pick out how each one had been done, which was absolutely fascinating to a kid.

Did my mother approve? Not really, but as long as I knew these films weren't real, then she tolerated it. I watched a ridiculous amount of horror between 12-13, and I am yet to become a serial killer (no matter how tempting it may become during day-job hours sometimes).

The videos themselves seemed huge to me back then, such was the size of the large format clamshell boxes in my young hands, and there was an atmosphere to the place which made those tapes seem taboo, dangerous, exciting. That was the allure of horror movies and the action films of the era, and it is an allure which still drives me to seek out more of them from those days. There is definitely an element of nostalgia for me and my quest, but there is also the point that if I don't rescue these films, then they may be thrown away and lost forever.

There was something grimy and seedy about the shops on that upper level, a little dangerous and a little scary, thanks to the gangs and drunks who would hang around at either end of that level and the strange people who both worked in those places and frequented them. That was my own version of the famous Grindhouse cinemas over in the USA. This was my 42nd street (just with marginally less tramp semen). Awful yet exhilarating.

Passing by the place on a recent visit back to my home town, all traces of those shops are long gone, erased in the council's slow, ponderous crawl towards renovating the area, which has now been going on for about fifteen years. I just wish my memory of the place was clearer. I wish I knew its name, or where the people who ran it went. I remember those racks of scary and exciting video tapes on shelves that were difficult to reach very clearly, and viewing the many films I bought from there all these years later, I remember the thrill of those early days of my endless genre film hunt. There's magic in those memories, and still magic for me in the films I collect and enjoy to this day.

Car boot sales are another avenue I have always enjoyed in the eternal search for VHS horror movies. For the uninitiated, or indeed anyone outside the UK, Car Boot Sales are public markets where any old junk is sold on tables and from the boots (aka trunk) of cars in fields, car parks or waste ground. They happen on a regular basis all over the country, and they are a fertile hunting ground for collectors of all kinds of memorabilia. You really don't know what you'll find and where. Of course, what you will usually find at Car Boot Sales is a selection of soiled underwear, odd shoes, model boats, home-made chutneys apparently made of family vomit samples, knackered vinyl records of 12" disco tunes, cages of dead pets, mouldy Danielle Steele paperbacks and mirrors with seashells stuck around them.

However, sometimes you will strike gold. Amidst all the random old shit people sell for 50p, you will often find little stashes of brilliance. VHS tapes are common on these sales, and there are sometimes some delights to be found. Amongst all the old Friends TV series videos, you will find a lot of Ex-rental tapes, including some very weird and obscure titles, which you can pick up for pennies. As a collector of other stuff too, I often walk away from these sales with armfuls of comics and sci-fi pulps too, along with a big stupid grin.

Car Boot Sales can either be the greatest thing in the universe or a monumental letdown when you're trying to find old horror movies, but that's part of the charm of the hobby – unless you find them specifically on eBay, Amazon or elsewhere online, then you really never know where the next tapes will show up, and that's kinda exciting.

I swear I have a lady. A wife, even. Reading that back, it would be easy for it to sound ridiculously sad to most people, but to a diehard VHS collector, these places are goldmines.

The most common places I hunt for VHS treats are charity shops, though. Charity shops have been very good to me indeed when it comes to filling my shelves with more and more films most people I know have never heard of/don't care about. That's another thing about VHS collectors – we LOVE a lot of crap everyone else hated. Is it something to do with some strange kitsch value? The rarity of the tapes? The value to other collectors? Possibly all of those, really.

For me, I love finding obscure horror movies on VHS because I long for an era of cinema that I could relate to. For a couple of years I even worked for a bunch of indie film companies, so my love for cheap special effects and lousy production values deepened yet further. The era of home cinema in which the low budget filmmakers found their feet and got their product out to audiences with an absolutely miniature fraction of Hollywood budgets was something I felt a great kinship with. You have to admire anyone with the dedication and nous to actually get a product out there for consumption, rather than just claiming "I could do better than that" whenever something doesn't appeal to them.

Anyway, as collectors of something which is becoming more and more difficult to find in the wild, we must look wherever we can for our fix. There are only a finite number of VHS tapes out there to be found in various places, and only a small number of those are horror tapes, so when the real world runs low on goodies for us to discover, snap up, watch, catalogue and fetishize over, then where do we go?

Online. Where else?

BUYING HORROR VHS ONLINE

The internet is a great place for many things, but it can also end up costing collectors fortunes both big and small. With eBay and Amazon (and other, smaller sites) showing us so many delights 24 hours a day, it's hard not to get caught up in buying anything and everything you want.

Before you know it, a brief buying binge has suddenly cost you a huge sum of money (not always on the tapes themselves, more on the postage and suchlike), and while your shelves will fill with more delights of a tape-based nature, your bank account will suffer like the guy in *Day of the Dead* who gets ripped to bits on that hydraulic platform.

Buying tapes online, be they from auction or retail sites or from private collectors, can be a tricky business. Due to the nature of the medium and the age of the items themselves, you really do need to pay attention to photos and listings, and ask various questions of the seller if you're not sure about anything.

A few points to consider are; Does the tape work? Is there tape mould (the white powdery substance) visible on the tape?

What condition is the sleeve/box/label in? What cut of the film is it? How has it been stored?

It's easy to get duped when buying VHS online if you don't check the state the tape is in, or indeed make sure the seller isn't a liar/maniac/nazi/Justin Bieber fan. Examine the photos and ask questions. Don't just buy blind, or you may lose a bunch of cash. There are some nice and easy tricks to finding decent tapes cheap on eBay and suchlike – just vary how you search for them.

On several occasions I've found some absolute treasures on there for next to nothing which were listed badly. Just by searching with simple terms like 'horror videos' or 'VHS horror' I found that a lot of people had put up batches of tapes with no further description, meaning that anyone searching for individual films wouldn't necessarily come across them, thus allowing you to pick them up for very little outlay.

This is a bit of a gamble, as you don't want to ask too many questions about those lots or people will wise-up to the fact they have some good stuff in those cheap batches. I prefer to pay small amounts for tapes rather than large sums, for two reasons. For one, I'm poor, and second, I'm not stupid.

Tapes going for massive amounts are a rare occurrence, and these sales are rarely indicative of a tape's quality. It's usually a case of a tape being very scarce, someone being a completist, or collectors having a fight over stuff. We're like that. The point is, there are millions of tapes out there to be found, but not all of them are as great as they may seem. They may be bootlegs, damaged, or just filled with movies so bad even I can't sit through them. Mind you, that would have to be really, REALLY bad...

SELLING HORROR VHS ONLINE

Selling tapes on the internet is pretty much an essential part of the hobby right now. The video tape market has blossomed in recent years, although some collectors feel that our niche interest is now too big, and thus prices are going up. The fact is, a tape is worth what a person is willing to pay for it. When I sell tapes online I tend to start my auctions off very low, usually at 99p. I figure if people want to pay more then they are welcome to bid the tapes up, but I don't want to rip off other collectors. Tapes rarely cost me much anyway, so I figure that I shouldn't try and fleece others like me for the stuff they need to get their next VHS fix. After all, those may well be people you'll end up buying tapes from in the future, so it's common courtesy, really.

Of course, there are tapes that need to be put up at a higher price, not just because they're liable to bring you in some more cash, but also because they need to be appreciated by more serious collectors. I mean, you don't want a copy of *Absurd* or *Nightmare Maker* or *Dreamaniac* or *Demon Queen* something similar falling into the hands of a passing-interest collector who will watch it once and then ignore it. So price things according to their value, of course, but make sure that value is sensible.

When selling your tapes on eBay or suchlike, make sure you are honest about what you are selling. Fill the listing with all of the good points about the film and how collectable it is, but make sure you also list the defects with the cover, any marks on the sleeve, how the tape plays, the condition of the cassette itself, the label and suchlike. If there is damage, then make sure that damage is noted in the listing, preferably with a photo. Real collectors, real enthusiasts and lovers of the format and the films will appreciate it. The tapes will still sell, and you will avoid negative feedback on your profile as well as avoiding a reputation as an arsehole.

Be clear in your descriptions. Mention the film, the edition, the condition, your postage rates and suchlike. Make sure you are honest. Collectors will be able to spot a lie a mile off. And ensure your tapes are genuine and not bootlegs. If you are concerned that a tape may be a bootleg copy, then don't try and sell it on an auction site as you risk ruining your account. Save those tapes to be traded on forums and in groups (but always make sure your fellow trader is aware that it is/might be a boot).

Add a sensible postage charge – don't try and suck cash out of people for postage. Once you have sent a few tapes out, you'll know what to charge to make sure the postage and materials you have used are covered. Don't try and bump up the money you get by upping the postage – it's transparent and will turn buyers away.

The main thing to do first though is to look around at what other people have for sale themselves. See how they do it, how they have listed things and how their descriptions and photos differ from your own. If someone else is selling similar tapes as you and are making more on them, then see what you can change about your own listings in order to improve them.

Above all, selling tapes online (to me, at least) is mainly a way to keep the hobby and scene alive rathe than just making cash. Of course, it's brilliant to make some coinage on a tape you didn't pay much for, but the main source of pleasure should be the continued dealings with other collectors.

HOW TO PACK VHS TAPES

Once you've sold or traded a tape, you need to send it out as quickly as you possibly can to the buyer/fellow trader. Speed is good, but not at the detriment of the packaging you use. You need to get it out there or risk bad feedback on eBay/Amazon/whatever, but if you're trading or selling directly to another collector, then you want to avoid getting a reputation as untrustworthy.

One aspect a lot of people get very wrong is the issue of how to package a tape up properly to send out. I will get this out of the way before I go further: Sticking a tape in a Jiffy bag/other padded envelope is NOT ACCEPTABLE. The tape will arrive damaged pretty much every time, and you will be seen as an idiot, cancelling out the possibility of future trades with other collectors. Right, that said, let's talk about how to do it the right way. Well, ONE of the right ways.

There are many techniques people use to properly package a tape up so that it arrives at its new home in good condition, and I have seen some genius uses of boxes, packing material and even wallpaper being used to secure tapes, but for the purposes of this book I'll tell you how I do this myself. It may seem mundane, but making sure that tapes arrive minty fresh and ready to be admired is just as important as the way you sell them, if not more. After all, you want people to come back for more, don't you? I thought so.

And thus here is a chapter in tape and cardboard. I worked a comic shop for nine years (which you can read about in a book entitled BAGGED AND BOARDED: LIFE ON PLANET GEEK), and we had a very busy mail order department which taught myself and every other wage slave there how to pack things very well indeed, so I do have a bit of experience in this field in addition to over a decade of selling on eBay.

Step One: Preparing the tape

First you need to get the tape ready to be sent out to your fellow collector. Make sure the tape has been tested, it works and that it is fully rewound and ready to be enjoyed once it arrives at its destination. This is just common courtesy, really.

Ensure the tape is in the box and it's the right tape. This last point may seem silly, but how annoying would it be to have the wrong thing arrive? Ensure the tape and case are in the condition you stated when selling it. Right. On to the packaging.

Step Two: The first layer of protection

I like to wrap the tapes I sell in a plastic supermarket carrier bag first of all. This adds little in the way of protection against knocks, but minimises any risk of the sleeve or art being scratched in the package in transit. It also helps to ensure the case doesn't try and open up or let the tape slip out.

Step Three: Padding

Once the tape is securely wrapped, we move onto additional padding. this is where I generally add a layer or two of bubble wrap and tape it around the bagged-up tape. If I haven't had bubble wrap to hand then in the past I have wrapped them in cardboard or bolstered the package with scrunched-up newspaper or spare wrapping paper. This is the first layer of padding.

Step Four: Boxing up your tape

If you're selling more than one tape, chances are that they won't fit through a letterbox, and as such you can go the whole hog with those and stick them (wrapped, of course) into a larger box and fill that with packing material. Sending individual tapes is more tricky, as you need to construct a box around the tape. That's the way I do it.

Using the large panels from the sides of a cardboard box, I will cut a length which can be wrapped around the tape's protected state nice and snugly. Secure this with parcel tape. Cut top and bottom lids from the spare cardboard and affix these onto either end of the package with more tape. Once the sides and lids are secure, add parcel tape to all of the edges, sealing the tape in a VHS sarcophagus.

Step Five: Finishing Up

Once the tape is sealed and safe, apply a clean label (I prefer to affix a separate label instead of writing on the box. Either use a good sized sticky label or attach a piece of clean paper with tape. Clearly write the address out on the label, add a return address on the rear of the package and affix FRAGILE stickers or tape, or just write it on as well. I like to write *Please Handle With Care – Thanks!* On my packages as I find that my tapes arrive in good condition if I treat the postal service like actual people rather than slaves. It seems to have worked for me so far. Make sure you leave space for the postage stamps or stickers, too.

Basically, look after the tape, protect it, pack it securely and send it out in a professional manner and other collectors will greatly appreciate it.

WHAT KIND OF COLLECTOR?

I guess I would say I'm an average collector when it comes to VHS horror. My collection is amazing to me, but it doesn't contain much which could be said to be particularly rare or valuable. I leave those tapes to the more hardcore collectors with a larger bank balance (or at least a healthier PayPal balance). First and foremost, my focus as a collector is the video rental shop I have in my head, meaning I'm mainly after copies of tapes I used to rent or wanted to rent back in the day.

Does this make the hobby an issue of nostalgia for me? Of course it does. I'd say most hobbies have an element of nostalgia to them, but tape collecting for me also has a kind of historical element to it. I really do feel that collectors and enthusiasts such as myself are helping to preserve the memory of an era which was massively influential for many years, but which now is seeming as archaic as wax cylinders or a Zoetrope. That's probably a very pretentious way of looking at it, but hey, I'm good at being pretentious, otherwise I wouldn't be constantly fighting back the urge to yell "Your new films are shit!!! Check these old-school titles out!"

I guess there is certainly an element of enjoying watching stuff a lot of other people have never heard of. It makes those titles seem more precious, more personal. I realise that makes me sound like a giant hipster, but rest assured, I wear socks, don't have a comedy beard or any crap sailor tattoos or ironic clothes. My interest in VHS is directly linked to the films themselves, rather than the monetary value of the tapes.

There are many films which I enjoy a great deal more on VHS than any other format. DVDs and suchlike are brilliant creations, but they feel impersonal, less tangible than a VHS tape with a chunky box and the pleasure of hearing the tape go into the machine and spool up, ready to play. As a collector, I guess I'm pretty rubbish in that case. Well, I'm sure I seem that way to some other collectors, whose shelves are bulging with ultra rare titles they don't really give a toss about beyond what they can get for them on eBay.

Don't get me wrong, I'm all for making a bit of cash out of tapes, but the love for the films and the format has to be there in the first place, not just an interest in making some cash out of gullible people with more money than sense. I like to find tapes in the wild and sell them on if I already have them or know that other people will enjoy them more. I like to think that by doing this, I'm getting tapes back onto the market which might otherwise vanish. One man's trash, and all.

I collect tapes for myself because I love the feel of them, love the act of watching a VHS movie, love the era they were popular and the cinematic delights of budgets both tiny and huge. I'll never be one of the big collectors, as I don't have the money or the inclination, really. I just want to collect stuff I like.

VHS AS 'THE NEW VINYL'

I've heard this mentioned a few times recently, this idea of VHS tapes being the new vinyl records in terms of being vintage collectibles, and I'm not entirely sure what to make of it. On one hand I completely agree, as these items are indeed from another era of popular culture and as such are going to be sought out by likeminded people to those who seek out rare vinyl.

On the other hand, I feel that the distinction pigeonholes VHS collectors as a certain type of person. I mean, the VHS collectors I know are pretty damn cool people, with jobs, partners and lives beyond the hobby itself. Plus, likening them to vinyl also brings the dreaded hipsters to mind again; The people into whatever 'Retro' fad is in season, who will pick anything up which they can laugh at and feel superior to. Those people can fornicate off, to be quite frank. For the majority of VHS collectors, this is something we've been doing for years, with its roots deep in the pages of our own life stories.

It's not an ironic, twee, 'vintage is like so kewl' thing to us. It's what we do. We talk about labels and sleeves and cut boxes and minty fresh tapes like old friends, not like people laughing at the funny-looking old analogue media encased in black plastic. Hipsters not allowed, thanks very much. This stuff is ours, and it means more than just some brief fad. So there.

Speaking of hipsters... Something which concerns a good few collectors on the scene of late is the recent upsurge in interest in VHS from that demographic. That is, people who aren't actually all that interested in VHS for its historic or nostalgic value, rather people who are getting into it because of the obsession with all things 'retro' and 'vintage' which has grown over the past decade or so.

This leads to some interesting debate amongst collectors, and of course some pretty entertaining flame-wars, too. One one hand it's cool that other people are finding out about the hobby and stating to enjoy a dead format again, but on the other hand the involvement of these people can be seen as muscling in on our territory, snapping up stuff that won't necessarily be appreciated properly or simply causing prices to rise across the board for the hobbyists out there.

I mean, once someone gets wind that VHS tapes are cool and 'the new vinyl' or whatever claim is being floated this week, then prices are naturally going to rise to meet the greed of sellers and the demand of the new audience. I'm somewhere in the middle with my opinion. I think it's cool that other, younger people are discovering the hobby and finding cool stuff to enjoy, but I do think that the trend-followers may get in the way of the real collectors.

Out of those fad-hooked kids I believe there are some great collectors and vintage film enthusiasts waiting to be developed and nurtured. However, the hobby can be very elitist at times and this can put some people off joining in the fun.

On rare occasions you will find a collector who is determined to make a point/spoil the fun for others by driving up the prices of tapes available online by crafty bidding on eBay and thus creating a false sense of worth for a lot of tapes. This in turn ends up with the cascade effect of tapes which were relatively cheap suddenly rocketing in so-called value.

I've witnessed this once first hand, when one collector was outed as a notorious eBay bidder who never won auctions but would always bid them up. This led to a great deal of conversation, debate and mud-slinging amongst the collector community regarding the effects this practice would have on the hobby, and which body part the bidder would be stuffed with first.

I do see the argument on both sides, but I believe that the scene is big enough for serious new collectors and enthusiasts to join in the fun and games while VHS tapes are still out there at low prices in the wild, and the Hipsters will fall by the wayside, hopefully getting rid of their trendy retro videotapes at a cut-price online for the rest of us to enjoy.

Sometimes it does feel like a case of 'Us Vs Them', the two sides being the old-school collectors like myself who grew up with these things and love them dearly, and the other being the cynical retro-nuts sniffing out stuff they can make some cash on.

But seriously folks, trends pass quickly enough, and once the current 'outsider' interest in cult VHS tapes passes, the scene will revert back into the hands of bitter old farts like me once again. Hang in there, folks.

COLLECTING HORROR VHS

Something you have to get used to as a VHS collector in this day and age is a lot of strange looks from people. Mind you, I get a lot of strange looks from people anyway, so I really shouldn't notice it at all by now. People tend to do a bit of a double take when I ask in charity shops and second hand stores if they have any VHS hidden away I can have a rummage through. "You want WHAT? Why would you want those?"

Explaining that I'm a collector doesn't help much either, leaving them with the impression of me as some form of deranged trainspotter. I often don't tell them much more than that, as if you give too much away, then people will automatically start to wonder if they should pit their prices up, lest something be more valuable than they originally thought.

This is apparently becoming a common problem for US collectors, who keep finding that in Goodwill stores and suchlike, it is becoming common practice for collectors to see staff checking the price of things on eBay before letting people buy them.

This is abhorrent, really, as not only does it make these people seem like utter arseholes, it also drives up the cost of a hobby which, for a time, was very cheap to enjoy. Some other things you may hear when you are a VHS horror collector may include:

- "Oh God, VHS? They were rubbish, weren't they?"

- "Why would you want them? They don't even make them any more..."

- "I've got a load of VHS tapes at home in the loft. Are they worth anything?"

- "Horror films? I like horror films. Like *SAW* and *Final Destination*..."

That last one irks me far more than it should, as I fully understand that horror here and now has been defined by such low quality material. Trying to explain to outsiders the visceral and cerebral beauty of something like *Suspiria* or *The Exorcist*, or the gonzoid fun of films like *Street Trash* or *Brain Damage* isn't easy when the other person has a frame of reference which is limited to crap torture porn movies, remakes of Japanese films or lowbrow teenage chillers (which are basically *Point Horror* stories with swearing).

Collecting horror VHS is a pastime which has provided me with a great deal of enjoyment, nostalgia, entertainment, information and more. Hell, I've built friendships, made (and lost) a bunch of money and enjoyed a heck of a lot of films. It's about as niche as it gets when it comes to hobbies, but I love it and it;s mine. I love that feeling, Collecting horror VHS felt like something only I did for such a long time, and finding other collectors was a weird experience indeed. More on those people later.

Being a VHS collector, or indeed any sort of collector, can make you seem a little odd to outsiders, but who cares? We're enjoying the hobby and enjoying sharing our passion for the format and an era of cinema with likeminded souls around the world, so leave us the hell alone. And no, your battered copy of *Elm Street 4* or *Aliens* or *Jerry Maguire* is worth nothing, so stop bugging me. Cheers.

DISPLAY IS KEY

The proper display of a good collection is a great sign of a genuine collector. If the tapes are stashed away in the loft or in a cupboard, you know there is a distinct lack of badassery going on in that house. However, if they are displayed loud and proud on rows of shelves and made into something of a focal point in a room, then it's clear the collector has put some serious time, cash and attention into gathering those tapes. Plus, the way in which a collection is displayed can tell you even more about a person.

I do feel that any collection, be it VHS tapes of obscure horror movies, books, comics or whatever, has a certain autobiographical quality to it. Most collectors will be able to tell you where they found favourite tapes, or how they sought hem out if he film has been special to them in some way.

These things are more than just little chunks of entertainment - they are relics of earlier days, and I know that for myself a lot of tapes have a connection to a time and place where my life was very different. They're like relays to the past, checkpoints that evoke younger days.

Of course, they're also fantastically entertaining too, which is the point, really. Hence, you will find collectors with their stash displayed in all manner of different ways, and not always alphabetical. A lot of people like to group them by distributor, or maybe genre, or box size, or even director. It's up to the individual, but I always find it fascinating to see how others have displayed their treasures.

Right now, my own collection is displayed in the main bedroom of our house, which is where it will remain until we can afford to have the library extension built. They are displayed on two large bookcases. The main core of my collection, namely my favourite horror tapes, are on a case by themselves. On top of that case is a pile of vintage horror magazines, a row of my absolute favourite tapes, stuff like *Trick Or Treat, The Video Dead, Neon Maniacs, Return of the Living Dead,* and a framed one-sheet poster for the aforementioned 1986 horror/metal/comedy movie *Trick Or Treat.*

Next to that is the secondary tier of my collection, namely another case where most of my other tapes are. This is a mixture of sci-fi, some common horror, comedy and general film releases. The top of the case contains no VHS, but instead has a stack of 80s metal vinyl, some action figures, rock and metal cassettes and a few boxed figures (you can take the geek out of the comic shop, but you can't take the comic shop out of the geek, sadly). Looking over these is an original video advertisement poster for the first *Nemesis* movie. God I love that poster image.

It's not a permanent home for my stash, but it suffices for now, and gives me a little corner of analogue geekery to indulge in. My collection is relatively small when compared to a lot of collectors, some of whom have entire rooms dedicated to films, and you have no idea how much I envy that.

I dream of having just such a room, which I can fill with old movies, posters in frames, a big fat old tube TV, shelves of old horror mags and a battered armchair. See, I aim high in life, don't I? Pardon me a moment while I sigh a bit.

Anyway, displaying a collection of VHS horror movies where everyone can damn well see them is a very cool thing to do. I did have mine in our living room, but we're in the middle of shifting the house around and thus my badassometer is running low. Seeing those rows of films laid out neatly, embellished with a sane amount of collectibles and ephemera, makes me very happy indeed. I find a great deal of pleasure in things looking orderly, and bookshelves full of films (or indeed books, considering the dozen bookcases in our house) can really put a stamp on a place. Don't hide those tapes away - flaunt those bad boys.

ON THE HUNT

Actively going on the hunt for tapes in the wild is a wonderful way to spend a day for an avid horror VHS collector. For one thing, it gets you out into the world and thus robs people of the chance to accuse you of watching TV all the time, and another, it opens up the country around you as a fertile new hunting ground to find new delights that you may otherwise miss. Of course, there are hunts which are total busts, but still, you get to see different places and experience more.

Being in the UK, I don't have thousands of miles of country to explore, unlike my US friends who collect tapes, and such my rare hunts out of town are limited to where I can easily get to by train. I don't drive, and as such am at the mercy of where public transport is able to take me. This can be a pain, but it does mean I can travel light, leaving me free to pick up tapes and not worry about finding a place to park and so on.

Going on a hunt in another city requires a little research before setting off, otherwise you could end up wandering around for hours without a single lead. Have a look round online at what people say about the place you're going.

Look up where the video shops used to be, and where the most charity shops are located. Look up any second hand shops or odd places selling curios. Maybe even some antique shops. I say this as I found a copy of Lucio Fulci's classic *House By The Cemetery* in an antique shop recently and paid next to nothing for it.

But the whole point is that the hunt should be fun. Explore places and seek those things out. Don't just rely on eBay and Amazon for your fix. Get out there into the world and visit places that have been forgotten by the march of time. Seek out the weird and wonderful in places just as weird and wonderful. You really don't know what you'll find out there. Granted, a lot of the time you'll find nothing at all, or the occasional kinda rare tape, but every now and then you will find something monumental. The tapes you find may not be particularly valuable, but that's not really the point of collecting them is it? The central motivation of collecting is to COLLECT, not sell on, and while even I do sell tapes on that I know people want more than I do myself, I don't just go out there to find stock for my eBay account. The hunt is on, so get out there and find that buried treasure.

However, the hunting grounds are starting to vanish. In the last few months, I've lost two of my favourite hunting spots for rare and weird VHS tapes, and this is a saddening trend which seems to be picking up around the world. It was always inevitable that the supply of cheap and ignored tapes would start to dry up eventually, and while there are still plenty out there to be found, the number of locations is dwindling.

The two places I lost recently were both fine examples of paradise to people like me. One place was a weird little second hand books, magazines and comic shop run by one guy, just outside the city centre on a street otherwise populated mainly by international food stores selling baskets of knobbly fruits and lethal hot sauces.

I miss it. I spotted it in passing one day while out exploring when we had first moved to Nottingham. It was closed at the time, but windows full of second hand science fiction books, music magazines and comic posters told me it was a place I should spend some time. I told my lady, Claire, about it (she's also a sucker for secondhand books, one if the many things I love about her, aside from her superhuman ability to put up with me), and we agreed to pay the place a visit the next time it was open.

We did so, and upon pushing the door open we were greeted by the unmistakable and wondrous smell of old books. I walked in and found an awesome selection of science fiction paperbacks, classic comics, music and film magazines, and a stack of assorted VHS tapes and DVDs. I was in heaven. I pulled out a bunch of 1980s metal magazines, some paperbacks and a couple of VHS tapes.

My other half didn't find anything of interest due to the geeky leanings of the stock, but she was happy to be amongst old books nonetheless. The thing that excited me was that the VHS tapes had a few obscure gems amongst them, so I knew I would be calling in often.

While Claire browsed the few sections that interested her, I marched proudly to the counter to pay for my finds. The guy who ran the place was, upon first glance, frighteningly creepy, gaunt and twitching. He was eyeing my other half with a mixture of lust and anxiety, as though a woman had never stepped into the shop before. She came over to join me at the counter, having exhausted the shelves she was looking at.

That's when we noticed all the porn.

The first glance was at the counter where the guy was bagging up my purchases. The whole table top of the counter was stacked with piles of aged porn mags, and we were struck with the notion that we couldn't see the guy below chest level. Was he wearing any trousers? Had we actually walked into his dusty den of printed filth while he was in the middle of shaking hands with the veiny love god? I exchanged a glance with Claire which stated that giggles would be had once we left. And possibly some hand sanitizer.

And then I looked to my left and saw the rest of the porn. Lots of it.

Hidden away behind a discreet wooden wall was a wonderland of wanking material from the 70s to the present day. Magazines, paperbacks, VHS, DVDs, contact mags and all manner of other vintage rudeness. We exchanged an awkward glance and then realised No Trousers Man was grinning like Gollum. A hasty retreat was beaten, lest any fluids erupt forth in my lady's direction. But it was okay. All was fine. I had found a new VHS hunting ground. I went back many times (however Claire didn't, for some odd reason) and picked up a good few other tapes from there along with myriad 80s metal and science-fiction magazines.

One day I went in there with hopes of VHS treats but found the place in even more disarray than usual. Gollum told me the place was closing down and he was switching to running an eBay shop instead. On one hand it was a relief as I wouldn't have to breathe in stale flakes of dried semen from the air, but on the other it meant a prime location for vintage collectable VHS tapes and cult magazines and comics was disappearing. Another one fallen by the wayside.

The other one was a different kind of store, more music than anything else, but it was just as cool. Not all that far away from Gollum's place, it specialised in vintage records plus DVDs and CDs, along with weird collectibles at the back of the shop. Typewriters. Old books. Strange antiques. Dolls. Toy robots. Badges. Assorted junk. I used to go in there and pick up cheap rock, metal and industrial CDs at first, but then I discovered the magic staircase...

At the back of the place, hidden amidst the old books, boxes of used postcards, creepy dolls and strange paraphernalia there was a staircase that would lead you into the cellar. I'd call it a basement room, but it was so dingy and musty that it could only really be called a cellar. Windowless and lit by bare bulbs, the cellar was a wonderland for obscure bargain hunters like myself.

The sole attempt at decoration was a large piece of wood, possibly from the side of an old wardrobe, which had dozens of actions figures nailed to it. Yeah, NAILED. Like the prized butterflies of some crazed bug collector, just with old G.I. Joe and He-Man figures. The price point was 20p. For anything. Books, records, CDs, magazines... and VHS tapes.

It was a massive amount of fun to rummage through those piles and boxes and cupboards of random thing, pulling out some gems in the process. Despite risking lung infections thanks to the poisonous air down in that cellar, the 20p cellar was thoroughly enjoyable and most fruitful. The first time I was in there I was accompanied by two vinyl freaks who were furiously thumbing through pile upon pile of discarded records. I found some weird paperbacks and a small stack of VHS tapes to silence my cravings for a while. They weren't in the best of condition, but hell, it was basically a load of forgotten shit in a cellar, what should I have expected?

But of course, nothing weird lasts as long as it should, and when I went there for another fix one day I found it boarded up, graffiti already daubed across the wood. The place was empty and gone.

This is a trend which is picking up speed. Weird little places are vanishing even quicker than major chains at the moment as a direct result of the continued domination of places like Amazon and eBay. Perhaps in some ways our own greed and demand as collectors is robbing us of the grassroots places which gave rise to the hobby in the first place. Supporting these places isn't always easy though due to the fluctuating stock they can get hold of, and thus it's understandable that our attention will turn to eBay and suchlike, but it's impossible to deny that right now, the hunting grounds are dropping in number.

Will this make the hunt more fun, or will it eventually harm the scene? I would say that VHS collecting is a hobby which has a limited lifespan as the generations the format meant a lot to continue to age and circumstances change, so enjoy those weird little places while you can. These are the days we'll remember in years to come when the tapes finally dry up.

Remember the weird and the strange and the musty air. Just try to blot out the guys who may not have had their trousers on.

THE LOWER THE BUDGET, THE MORE I LOVE IT

Something that the rise of the VHS era gave way to was a gigantic boom of low budget filmmaking where the usual constraints of Hollywood studio films didn't apply. There was less money, sometimes almost no money at all for the companies and crew making indie movies back then, and thus a lot of the studio involvement didn't apply. This allowed for a greater artistic streak in some films, an anarchic sense of chaos in others, or absolutely no production values or entertainment value in the very worse examples.

Two companies which held my imagination with their low-budget trash epics were the inimitable Troma and the iconic (To me, anyway,) Full Moon Productions (aka Full Moon Features, etc). Troma are legendary for their lack of cash and the utter mayhem of their own productions, and I maintain that it's almost impossible not to be entertained by early films like *Class Of Nuke 'Em High, The Toxic Avenger, Seargant Kabukiman NYPD* or their 90s masterpiece *Tromeo and Juliet*. The company, founded and run by Lloyd Kaufman (one of indie cinema's coolest – and most eccentric and opinionated - characters), is famed for its can-do attitude and the distinct style and humour of their films, and long may they continue to be trashy and wonderful.

Full Moon have a special place in my geek heart as they brought me some of my favourite ever VHS tapes, including *Puppet Master, Castle Freak, Arcade, Subspecies* and *Demonic Toys*. Prior to Full Moon, Charles Band ran Empire Pictures, which brought us joys like *Trancers, Metalstorm: The Destruction of Jared-Syn, The Dungeonmaster, Slave Girls From Beyond Infinity* and the joyously titled *Sorority Babes In The Slimeball Bowl-O-Rama*. There's a delightful comic- book feel to those eras of the company, which seems to have changed a little as they went from incarnation to incarnation of the business. I still love them, despite their faults. Head honcho Charles Band has a lot to answer for, namely making my teenage years rather more twisted. A lot of people have their issues with Charles and Full Moon, but I have a lot of nostalgia attached to the brand and as such still kinda like them.

Low budget movies are magical to me, even when they're utter crap like a lot of camcorder flicks which find their way onto cheap DVDs. I mean, you really have to admire the cast and crew for working for no money just to get a product finished and out there. I find that humbling, as I've worked for low budget film companies and next to nothing ever got finished, let alone released. It wasn't for lack of trying, I can tell you. However, these people have managed it, and I have a great deal of respect for that. The drive and the discipline needed to make a film is staggering, and doing one with pretty much no budget whatsoever is even more impressive.

There are so many things to deal with, the admin, the schedules, an unpaid cast, the effects, the lights, the stock, the locations, the transportation, food, drink, shelter, post-production, distribution and marketing along with everything else, that it astounds me more filmmakers aren't completely insane and trying to take an axe to anyone in sight. Granted, a lot of the admin and post-production and design can now be done at home on domestic computers (for example, the one I'm writing this on at home has more speed and power than any edit suite I ever worked with), but there is still an enormous amount of random crap to be dealt with throughout making a film.

For a long time during the rental years, I would actively look for stuff with a low budget and a cast I hadn't heard of. That is, unless it had Linnea Quigley, Brinke Stevens or Debbie Rochon in it, as those always got my money anyway back in the day.

One thing that has changed since then is the label Entertainment in Video, who back in the day was something of a bargain-bin distributor which has now developed into a big name over the years. Similarly I find it very interesting to see New Line

Cinema, the company that brought us Freddy Krueger in the *A Nightmare On Elm Street* movies, ended up becoming one of the biggest movie studios in the world for a while thanks to the gargantuan success of the epic big screen adaptations of *The Lord Of The Rings* and *The Hobbit*. The company was then absorbed by Warner Brothers. The name lives on, but the independence is gone.

    Of course, not many of the small studios have lasted, let alone thrived. It is tantamount to their business sense and output that companies such as Full Moon Troma have had such longevity. Those companies in particular stick out as having an understanding of their core audience, which is what has helped them stay in business all this time. That and a general air of stubbornness, which is to be admired in this day and age.

THE LURE OF THE VIDEO NASTIES

It's impossible to talk about loving horror movies on VHS and not talk about the infamous Video Nasties controversy, which is fine by me as I love talking about it. While the DPP's list of 72 'films that will corrupt the viewer' was designed to act as a guide of films that were too violent, too reprehensible for public consumption, all that really happened was that those films became even more notorious and sought after. In trying to ban those films, the powers-that-be simply turned them into something that people wanted even more than before, leading to piracy and the circulation of low quality bootlegs.

The simple fact is, a great many of the films on the DPP list were absolutely awful as flicks, but they contained a scene or two which went beyond the realms of good taste and thus wound up gaining a longevity far beyond their limited initial availability. I mean, come on, films like *The Beast In Heat, Forest Of Fear, Island of Death* and so on, are all very shoddily made and almost impossible to take seriously.

Case in point: In one scene during *The Beast In Heat*, a young lady is tied to a table and 'devoured by rats'. That sounds horrific until you see the actual thing and discover that the screaming victim merely has some fake blood on them... and two very docile looking guinea pigs. Seriously. The murderous, flesh eating rats are actually two bored guinea pigs sat on someone's stomach while they yell at the 'torture'.

A lot of the controversy surrounding the so-called Video Nasties stemmed from the use of extreme cover artwork, intended to draw potential viewers to the films on offer, as there was next to no budget available for distributors to market their wares. Thus, when lunatics like the late Mary Whitehouse (the self appointed "Moral guardian" of the British public back in the day) saw the cover to stuff like Ruggero Deodato's notorious *Cannibal Holocaust,* depicting a savage-looking character chewing on some messy entrails, all Hell broke loose.

Suddenly the horror movies coming out unrated from small distributors were being blamed for everything wrong with society, from murders and suicides to rape and pretty much every other crime at the time. Be it *Zombie Flesh Eaters*, *Unhinged, Anthropophagous The Beast* or any of others, they were seen as causing the downfall of the country's morality and the rising tide of violence.

At the time though, the was a general air of tension across the country due to massive unemployment, huge social unrest and a government who really didn't care about the actual people they were supposed to be leading. Looking back at that era now, it is plain to see that the films in the Video Nasties scare and subsequent witch-hunt were little more than scapegoats that were a convenient explanation for the evils of a country in turmoil.

The simple fact is that these films did not and do not corrupt society. Society was and is already corrupt to begin with, and now many of those films seem tame when compared to the 'torture porn' trend in so-called horror movies of the contemporary scene.

So what exactly is the lure of the Video Nasties? Why have so many people sought them out and fetishised them? One reason in particular is that many were banned outright, while others were banned and then later reintroduced to the market in edited versions, ergo making the original versions of those films taboo and intriguing by their definition as being too nasty for viewers to consume.

Now, the DPP's list acts as something of a shopping list for collectors, with the dozens of titles that still remain banned in their uncut form being highly prized items. A number of these films have never even been released on later formats such as DVD or Blu-Ray, making their original VHS editions that much more coveted. Furthermore, at the height of the controversy in the first part of the 1980s, a huge amount of tapes were confiscated and destroyed in huge furnaces, thus making any remaining copies even more rare.

Everything the government and outspoken do-gooders did to destroy and hold back those films just made people want them more. They were dangerous. They were powerful. They were essential. There was something frightening and exciting about those films thanks to so many people freaking out about their existence.

I got a taste of this as a teenager in the early 1990s, when a lot of films on the list which are now readily available were still banned. My cousin brought over a video for me to check out which contained bootleg copies of two films from the list, namely *The Exorcist* (don't forget, that film, for all its classic status and adulation, was banned for a long time – although it wasn't part of the DPP's Video Nasties list) and the far more grotesque (but nowhere near as well-made) *Anthropophagous The Beast*. He'd borrowed the tape off some guy at work and thought I'd be into it as he knew I already loved horror movies.

Just holding that unlabelled VHS tape was exciting, as we knew it held Things Which Should Not Be Seen within it. Slipping it into my player and discovering a third or fourth generation copy of each film on it was even more exciting. The bad picture and sound quality only added to the sense of danger and oncoming nastiness. The effects looked real through the static haze of the tape. It felt illicit and a little dirty, but thrilling. The films were a revelation.

The Exorcist was fascinating and scary and horrible, fully deserving of its iconic status, while *Anthropophagous The Beast* was a cheap and brutal movie about a bunch of people trying to escape a cannibal on a small island. The uncut version of the film, which is what I saw, included the infamous foetus-eating scene and the full ending, in which the titular cannibal eats his own innards as he dies. Those moments were foul and shocking, but made even worse by the low picture quality, which hid the cheap effects from greater scrutiny. That is one of the beauties of VHS horror – you often think you have seen more than you actually have. When viewing the same things on DVD or Blu Ray, the cheap effects and the joins in hastily applied prosthetics are all the more visible, which to me detracts from the film itself and reminds you what you're watching isn't real. Analogue media wasn't the best thing for films and music to be released on, but it certainly had a hell of a lot of atmosphere, and maybe the bad tracking and cheap copies made those films seem so much better than they really were. Either way, they ruled.

    The Video Nasties are a curious bunch of films, to be honest. There are some truly twisted flicks in there (*Nightmares in a Damaged Brain* - aka *Nightmare* in the US, comes to mind), but then there are also some which are just demented (*The Beast In Heat*, *Island Of Death* for example) or some which are just a bit dull (*Unhinged*, *Night Of The Bloody Apes*, *Snuff* etc). Without the notoriety given to them by those 72 films being banned, they have lived on far longer than their meagre budgets and initial takings suggested. I mean, a lot of the films on the list were made to be throwaway entertainment to capitalize on a burgeoning horror/sleaze boom, and are a long way from what anyone could call great art.

    Then again, there are films on the list like Dario Argento's *Tenebrae* or Lucio Fulci's *The House By The Cemetery* which are really quite wonderful, albeit wonderful in a grim, stylized vision of orchestrated violence and messy terror.

    I have always been a little annoyed that I wasn't born sooner, so I could have really taken part in that whole era of collecting, rental and controversy. I do remember it, but only as soundbites from news reports and suchlike of the era. I have since educated myself in the events of the era via books, magazines, documentaries and of course the films themselves. I know I'll never own a full set of the DPP's list, but that's okay, as some things are better left out there in the wild rather than on my shelves, otherwise there would be nothing left to search for.

The Video Nasties era happened at such an interesting time in British cultural history that it's hard for old-school horror fans over here not to crave those tapes and the uncut versions of those films, and quite rightly so. The fact that most of the films on that list (but not all of them) are now available legally here in fully uncut editions is both entertaining and sickening, as I can't help but think about the people who lost their livelihoods or ended up serving jail time for putting the films out there onto the market.

I find it ridiculous in the extreme that a stack of videotapes could be demonised to such a degree, but it did happen, and it was indeed a massive news at the time. The fact that newspapers were putting the films up there as the cause of the downfall of civilization is just as bizarre.

That the public went and found these films anyway, despite their apparent evil powers, tells you a lot about the interest which the controversy and political debate itself generated. Without that mania surrounding them, a great many of these films would be seen as nothing more than odd curios in the darkest recesses of film collector circles. As it is, they gained a mystique which often far outweighs their actual content.

The Video Nasties live on because they pissed a lot of stuck-up people off, and that's a brilliant legacy for them to have.

VIDEO NASTIES: THE FULL LIST

Presented here is a run-down of the full list of movies that wound up on the infamous Video Nasties list. This list of movies has, over the years, become something of a shopping list for VHS horror collectors who want to one day gather the full set. I cannot imagine just how much money and effort would go into that! Some are incredible, some are mediocre, and some are just painful to sit through. Many of the films are available at a discount on DVD or Blu Ray if you don't want to shell out for the originals.

Before we take a look at each film in alphabetical order, I must present two lists – the 'Final 39', otherwise known as the films which were prosecuted under the obscene publications act, and the 'Dropped 33' which were classed as video nasties but never prosecuted. The two lists are as follows:

The Prosecuted 39

Absurd
Anthropophagous: The Beast
Axe
The Beast in Heat
Blood Bath
Blood Feast
Blood Rites
Bloody Moon
The Burning
Cannibal Apocalypse
Cannibal Ferox
Cannibal Holocaust
The Cannibal Man
The Devil Hunter
Don't Go in the Woods
The Driller Killer
Evilspeak
Exposé
Faces of Death
Fight for Your Life
Flesh for Frankenstein
Forest of Fear
Gestapo's Last Orgy
The House by the Cemetery
The House on the Edge of the Park
I Spit on Your Grave
Island of Death

The Last House on the Left
Love Camp 7
Madhouse
Mardi Gras Massacre
Nightmares in a Damaged Brain
Night of the Bloody Apes
Snuff
SS Experiment Camp
Tenebrae
The Werewolf and the Yeti
Zombie Flesh Eaters

The non-prosecuted 33

The Beyond
The Bogey Man
Cannibal Terror
Contamination
Dead & Buried
Death Trap
Deep River Savages
Delirium
Don't Go in the House
Don't Go Near the Park
Don't Look in the Basement
The Evil Dead
Frozen Scream
The Funhouse
Human Experiments
I Miss You, Hugs and Kisses
Inferno
Killer Nun
Late Night Trains
The Living Dead at the Manchester Morgue
Nightmare Maker
Possession
Pranks

Prisoner of the Cannibal God
Revenge of the Bogey Man
The Slayer
Terror Eyes
The Toolbox Murders
Unhinged
Visiting Hours
The Witch Who Came From the Sea
Women Behind Bars
Zombie Creeping Flesh

Right. Onto the films themselves in alphabetical order. I do implore you to check out a good few of them. However, remember that original VHS copies of some of these titles will cost you a small fortune, or indeed a large fortune instead. Of course, most are available at affordable prices on various forms of digital media, but where's the fun in digital formats? Eh? Behold, the nasties...

ABSURD (1981)

Joe D'amato's sequel to the next film in the list, this was also known as *Monster Hunter, Horrible* and more. A crazed, self-regenerating lunatic stalks the inhabitants of a normal house. A sci-fi edge sits uneasily with the gory mayhem on show, but it does offer something a little different to what had already been done. Not as demented as the film which came before it, but far better made.
Status: The uncut film is still banned in the UK.

ANTHROPOPHAGOUS THE BEAST (1980)

Joe D'amato made himself notorious with this grisly (yet somewhat tedious) film about a group of people trapped on an island with a porridge-faced cannibal. The notorious foetus-eating scene has kept the film's reputation as a genuine Nasty intact. Worth seeing, but not the best film you could spend money on. Aka *The Grim Reaper.*
Status: Uncut version remains banned in the UK.

AXE (1974)
Also known as *Lisa, Lisa*, this slow-burning revenge movie takes a long time to get going, but once it does the horrific payoff is very satisfying. The film is very tense, if a little overly dramatic. However, that final act is great fun. The trailer is genius.
Status: Now available uncut.

BAY OF BLOOD (1971)
Thirteen murders carried out in thirteen increasingly inventive ways form the core of this grisly and surprisingly effective film, following the dastardly goings-on in order to get hold of the estate of a dead countess. Known under many titles (the most popular other title being *Twitch Of The Death Nerve*), *Bay of Blood* brought the work of Mario Bava to a much wider audience as well as the attention of the UK authorities, who saw fit to deem it too shocking to keep on the shelves. Viewed now it seems almost quaint, but still shockingly brutal and cruel in places.
Status: Now available in the UK uncut.

THE BEAST IN HEAT (1977)
Also known as *SS HELL CAMP* (and other titles), this is both one of the most valuable and scarce of the video nasties, but it's also one of the worst films of the bunch as well. Nazisploitation of the lowest order, it follows the exploits of a group of Nazi officers experimenting on innocent people in a secluded laboratory. Notable for Salvatore Baccaro as the titular beast, who spends the film naked and fornicating. Or eating pubic hair.

One scene of note aptly demonstrates the ineptitude of the production: A woman is being tortured and 'devoured by rats', but the crew couldn't get rats, so they used Guinea Pigs. Yes, Guinea Pigs. So there's the actress, screaming and writhing, naked apart from lashings of fake blood, and upon her sit two completely docile little piggies, looking nonplussed. A terrible film, but worth picking up if you find it cheap as it's worth a bundle.

Status: Remains banned for release in the UK

THE BEYOND (1981)

Arguably Lucio Fulci's greatest creation, *The Beyond* is a master class in surreal supernatural terror and visceral gore. Full of his trademark visual flare, it's also nightmarishly unsettling thanks to the disjointed nature of its non-linear plot. But who cares about plot when you have melting faces, the obligatory eye gouging scenes, much ripping flesh, truly unsettling zombies (A rarity in zombie movies) and such a gloriously downbeat ending?

The Beyond is brilliant and brilliantly horrific, although if you expect a straightforward horror movie, you will be sorely disappointed. For those who understand and appreciate Fulci's horror, it doesn't get much better than this.

Status: Now available uncut.

BLOOD FEAST (1963)

One of Herschell Gordon Lewis' infamous gore movies, *Blood Feast* is in fact considered to be the very *first* gore movie, its cheap-but-occasionally-effective makeup effects doing their job well and freaking out the self-righteous enforcers of so-called moral decency. A demented caterer uses hacked-up body parts in his dishes. Delicious.

Status: Now available uncut.

BLOOD RITES (1968)

Also known as *The Ghastly Ones*, this is a pretty standard piece of trashy horror cinema, with unwitting victims being offed in a variety of ways. Good fun, if rather unmemorable. I can't imagine why it hasn't been rereleased over here, as it's nowhere near as extreme as some people would have had you believe.

Status: No UK rerelease has been passed or released.

BLOODY MOON (1981)

Some truly awful special effects (refer to the monstrous saw blade killing in the trailer for proof) aside, *Bloody Moon* was a pretty effective slash and stalk movie from legendary genre director Jesus - aka Jess - Franco. Girls are being murdered at a language academy in Spain, but is the culprit really the disfigured lunatic freshly out of jail, or someone else?
Status: Now available uncut.

THE BOGEY MAN (1980)
A haunted mirror sets about murdering everyone that it can. A haunted mirror? Yeah, it sounds ridiculous, but while not the best film you could see, the mirror sequences are genuinely creepy. Visually weird, *The Bogey Man* has some scenes which really stick with you. It's just a shame the plot and acting are so flimsy.
Status: Now available uncut.

THE BURNING (1981)
Coming out after *Friday The 13th*, it's impossible not to compare The Burning to that far more popular film due to the very similar plot and pacing. However, to be honest I'd say *The Burning* is the better film. It's certainly more horrific and more effective. The Cropsy killer (when you finally see his visage) is a gloriously disturbing piece of makeup work from the legendary Tom Savini himself, and with the kill scenes on display throughout the movie it's easy to see why the DPP didn't take too kindly to it. A gem amongst the Video Nasties.
Status: Now available uncut.

CANNIBAL APOCALYPSE (1980)
A very different sort of cannibal movie to the more well known entries such as *Cannibal Holocaust* or *Cannibal Fox*, it is however arguably far better than both in terms of cast and production. John Saxon takes the lead as a Vietnam veteran who contracted a cannibalistic 'virus' during the war. Normal life hasn't been easy, and then a couple of other veterans arrive in the scene and reveal the cannibalistic violence that took them over in the past. The urban setting and disco soundtrack make it feel

more like an action movie than a straightforward horror, and as a result it is fabulously entertaining.

Status: Now available uncut aside from 2 seconds of animal cruelty.

CANNIBAL FEROX (1981)

Known to a lot of US collectors as *MAKE THEM DIE SLOWLY*, this riotously unpleasant exploitation flick from Umberto Lenzi is a good companion piece to Deodato's *Cannibal Holocaust* (see next entry) but not as good a film. The violence is there in spades (including the infamous hooks-through-the-boobs scene and the penis-being-hacked-off scene), but it lacks the social commentary aspect of *Cannibal Holocaust* (mind you, that was pretty flimsy too to be honest) and just goes for all-out exploitation.

Cannibal Ferox is one of the many infamous Italian movies of the time which starred John Morghen, aka Italian character actor Giovanni Lombardo Radice, who makes anything he's in ten times better. Not perfect, but suitably gruesome, and it's best viewed minus the needless scenes of animal cruelty, which I can't condone no matter how much I love exploitation movies and horror cinema.

Status: Not available fully uncut in the UK and several other countries.

CANNIBAL HOLOCAUST (1974)

Ruggero Deodato's cannibal epic is probably the most famous of all of the Video Nasties, thanks to its lurid cover art depicting a wide-eyed cannibal munching on some fresh entrails. Aside from the controversy surrounding the film, it is far a far better movie than you may initially expect. It used the 'found footage' trope which is now so common in genre fare decades before it showed up in *The Blair Witch Project, Cloverfield, REC,* the *Paranormal Activity* films and suchlike. In fact, it's that style of filmmaking which makes a lot of the special effects so convincing, as they are shown in a more real context. Hence the trouble the film ran into when some lunatics thought it was real. The simple and brooding soundtrack helps the atmosphere a great deal as well.

Yes, there are some truly grotesque moments of brutal violence (and some even more shocking 'aftermath' shots), but they add to the film's power and make it very effective as a chilling narrative. All I would take out of the film are the needless scenes of animal cruelty (never a good thing) and you are left with a flick which deserves both the notoriety and admiration that it has built up over the years.
Status: Still not available fully uncut in the UK.

THE CANNIBAL MAN (1972)
Despite the title, there are no scenes of cannibalism in the film. A pretty standard murder-based thriller with some sub-giallo gore moments. Nothing to write home about.
Status: Available almost uncut.

CANNIBAL TERROR (1981)
This French production is one of the most unconvincing of all of the Video Nasties. A poor rip-off of earlier cannibal movies (including some very 'similar' footage to that in Jess Franco's *Mondo Cannibale),* it's pretty much only notable now for the hilariously unconvincing cannibal tribe, most of who are clearly students or wannabe actors either blacked-up or daubed in comedy facepaint. One for completists only.
Status: Available uncut.

CONTAMINATION (1980)
This (figuratively and literally) messy science fiction horror movie features a number of exploding stomachs and other miscellaneous gore, stitched together by a wafer-thin plot about alien eggs which had been aboard a ship coming home from Mars. It's entertaining as long as you have cast-iron suspension of disbelief. When this was rereleased, the rating was lowered to a 15 certificate. And to think people had their livelihoods ruined over stuff like this which is now available to kids!
Status: Available uncut.

DEAD & BURIED (1981)

Something of an anomaly amongst the video nasties, *Dead & Buried* is a genuinely great film as well as being unsettling and horrifying. Something has gone awry in a picturesque town, in which the inhabitants may not be all that they initially seem. Some grisly murder scenes feature, but the most unsettling moment to me is the lengthy undertaker scene in which a young woman who dies in a bad way is skinned down to her musculature and then built back up to be beautiful for her funeral. The effects are chillingly convincing.

Written by *Alien*'s Dan O'Bannon and Ronald Shusett and stylishly directed by Gary Sherman, *Dead & Buried* plays like a gory episode of *The Twilight Zone* or like one of the legendary EC horror comics. Atmospheric, shocking and well constructed, this is certainly one of the better films on the DPP's list.

Status: Now available uncut.

DEATH TRAP (1977)

Tobe Hooper was never going to have an easy ride of it when trying to follow up the phenomenon that was *The Texas Chainsaw Massacre*. While this studio-bound tale of a lunatic running a tattered hotel going on a rampage and feeding people to an alligator has its moments, it is largely an I satisfying film experience. A few grisly scenes are on show, as is a young pre-Freddy Krueger Robert Englund, but this flick leaves me cold. I know that's got its fans (there's a good cult following in the US, under the title of *Eaten Alive* -not to be confused with Umberto Lenzi's film of the same name), but it feels too staged thanks to the blatant studio setting.

Status: Now available uncut

DEEP RIVER SAVAGES (1972)

Known to many as *The Man From Deep River, Deep River Savages* was pretty much the film that kick-started the Italian Cannibal genre in the eyes of many fans. Directed by Umberto Lenzi, the film is eminently watchable as a bit of exploitative 70s fun, but its not really violent or rude enough to warrant being part of the Video Nasties scandal. Sure, there are some tasty gore scenes and lots of gratuitous nudity from the notorious Me Me Lai as the central love interest alongside Ivan Rassimov's lead,

but scenes of real animal cruelty are probably what landed this film on the list. Take those out and you ave a pretty decent film.
Status: Available, but not fully uncut (missing only the scenes of animal cruelty, which is a fine omission as far as I'm concerned).

DELERIUM (1979)
A somewhat run-of-the-mill slasher movie for the first half, *Delirium* sticks out because of the scenes violence against women, and the film leaves a bit of a bad taste in the mouth. Inept and unpleasant (it feels like two films stitched together in a very shoddy fashion), it's one of the Video Nasties without a great deal to recommend within it. Hard to find and rather valuable, but also rather dull.
Status: Not currently available.

THE DEVIL HUNTER (1980)
Jess Franco was, at times, a genius. Sadly, he left his genius in a box somewhere while making this turgid cannibal-craze movie. It's currently an extremely expensive tape to own due to the scarce nature of the original copies in the first place, but that's no marker of quality. Thugs kidnap a girl and take her to a remote island, and are pursued there by two Vietnam veterans. Once there, they all terrorised by a hilarious looking zombie/cannibal dude with ping pong balls for eyes. Yeah, I'm not sure either.
Status: Available uncut.

DON'T GO IN THE HOUSE (1980)
This flick scared the crap out of me when I first saw it, although I did see it at an age when I really shouldn't have been watching horror movies. I revisited it as an adult and it still had the same power. One of the most disturbing of the Video Nasties in my opinion, *Don't Go In The House* follows a similar vein to Hitchcock's *Psycho*, but takes it to far nastier extremes.

A schizophrenic man erects a steel room in the house of his dead mother (whose corpse sits in front of the TV in the living room, screaming at the lead character in his head), into which he brings women he has drugged, in order to hang them by chains to the ceiling and barbecue them alive with a flame thrower. He then dresses the charred corpses up in his mother's clothes and sits them beside her remains as though having a grisly tea party.

His madness spirals out of control and finishes up destroying him in a weird but very effective ending. Some of the effects sequences have aged very well (the first time you see a full shot of a victim being torched is horrifyingly convincing), and the film remains a harrowing experience even for diehard horror fans.

Status: Available uncut.

DON'T GO IN THE WOODS (1981)

A 'trapped in the wilderness' slasher movie directed by James Bryan, *Don't Go In The Woods* (I always thought it was called *Don't Go In The Woods... Alone!* Due to the packaging) is a passable bit of exploitation cinema. There are plenty of gallons of fake blood squirting in all directions, all of which help to cover up the distinct lack of plot. While gory, it's not really gory enough or violent enough to warrant its place on the DPP's list, although those who seek it out will have a pretty rare tape in their collection.

Status: Available uncut and now with a 15 certificate.

DON'T GO NEAR THE PARK (1981)

What the? I have no idea. Some cave-dwellers have been killing people for 12,000 years and now want to break their curse via a virgin sacrifice. Gore, cannibalism and an appearance by the inimitable Linnea Quigley (See films like *Night of The Demons*, *Nightmare Sisters, Creepozoids* or a massive number of other flicks for proof of how cool dear Linnea is) can't save this mess of a film. I'm sure it has its fans, but it's just a bit too inept even more my tastes. The gut-munching was like a censorship magnet with this one.

Status: Now available uncut.

DON'T LOOK IN THE BASEMENT (1973)

I really enjoyed this flick, but its one of those that some will find hard to believe was seen as a video nasty. Literally a case of the lunatics taking over the asylum, a nurse starts work at a home for the insane and discovers that the staff have been done away with and the inmates rule the roost.

At times unintentionally hilarious, the film is still effective thanks to its wanton atmosphere of exploitation. It's cheap, nasty and odd, just how we like it. Bizarrely, the film has now been downgraded in the UK to a 15 certificate. How things change!

Status: Now available uncut.

DRILLER KILLER (1979)

Thanks to its unforgettable cover art depicting the movie's most famous scene, in which a hapless tramp has a drill shoved into his face, Abel Ferrara's *Driller Killer* found itself at the centre of the Video Nasties controversy. Unfortunately, aside from some memorable murder scenes, the film is remarkably boring, mainly showing footage of a really dodgy underground band rehearsing a few songs and arguing. Worth seeing for its notoriety, but not worth the controversy that stemmed from its cover.

Status: Now available uncut. Incidentally, this film is now considered to be Public Domain in the UK.

EVIL DEAD (1981)

Sam Raimi's seminal horror-comedy masterpiece was just begging to end up on a list like this, and it revels in both its extremity and its ridiculousness. An absolute joy to watch, *Evil Dead* is so over the top with its gore and creatures that it still beggars belief to this day. Yeah, the film is gory and violent, but its not a malicious film at all - more a celebration of the genre and of the gross-out moment.

Yes, its first sequel, *Evil Dead 2: Dead By Dawn* was a better film by far, but the original lives on in horror fans' hearts around the world for its sheer audacity and joyful atmosphere. Plus, it brought the world the talents of the awesome Mr. Bruce Campbell. Did it deserve its place on the Video Nasties list? Not really, but the people who put the list together were largely reactionary lunatics anyway.

Status: Now available uncut.

EVILSPEAK (1981)
This is a curious entry on the list as, like *Dead & Buried*, it is a really well made, well directed film with a great cast. Clint Howard takes the lead as Stanley Coopersmith, a military cadet who is constantly bullied by his peers. When the bullying finally goes too far, he utilizes computer programs and human blood in order to resurrect a Satanic cult leader who died 300 years earlier, who bestows upon him demonic powers. It's hard to see why *Evilspeak* got onto the DPP's list, until towards the end once the demented violence, beheadings, man-eating pigs and more are unleashed. It's hokey, but it's really well shot and well worth a look for any fan of 80s horror.
Status: Now available uncut.

EXPOSE (1976)
A writer suffering from paranoia, played by Udo Kier, is trying to finish a novel in a country house. The secretary he employs is raped, and he murders the two youths responsible. From there, all manner of sex, violence and insanity ensues. Not your standard horror fare, but suitably shocking. Uneasy viewing.
Status: Not currently available uncut.

FACES OF DEATH (1978)
This Mondo film (look up the Mondo movies and be freaked out/enthralled, depending on how your brain is wired up) is made up of a series of grotesque and at points deeply unsettling death scenes. According to someone involved with the film, about 40% of the scenes are fake (some very obviously are). While sought after by collectors, the scenes of animal killings are abhorrent.
Status: Not available uncut.

FIGHT FOR YOUR LIFE (1977)
Now here's an anomaly on the DPP's list. *Fight For Your Life* is an action movie about a black family held hostage by a redneck and his cronies. The violence isn't what got it onto the list – instead it was the language and attitudes in the film! A harrowing

and unbelievably racist film, it was only briefly available on video and never hit cinemas here.
Status: Not currently available in the UK.

FLESH FOR FRANKENSTEIN (1973)
Otherwise known as *Andy Warhol's Flesh For Frankenstein* as it was produced by the eccentric art legend, this flick is campy, gory, sexy and more than a little odd. Interesting as it was originally screened in a lot of markets in 3D, with some disembowelment scenes shot specifically so that innards are rammed at the camera.
Status: Now available uncut.

FOREST OF FEAR (1980)
Notable mainly for its utterly atrocious cut-and-paste job of a cover, *Forest of Fear* is also known as *Bloodeaters* and *Toxic Zombies*. Illegal plantations are sprayed with a chemical which turns a group of hippies into flesh-eating zombies. Its director, Charles McCrann, was sadly killed in the World Trade Centre attacks of September 11th, 2001.
Status: No rerelease available in the UK.

FROZEN SCREAM (1975)
This drug-fulled sort-of zombie movie follows a mad scientist who comes up with an immortality potion, and its subsequent nasty side-effects. More a trippy drug movie than a horror film.
Status: Not available on the UK market.

THE FUNHOUSE (1981)
An archetypal slasher movie, this kids-stalked-in-a-fairground-by-a-deformed-madman flick is entertaining enough, but why it ended up on the list is beyond me. Nothing is particularly extreme. In fact, this has since been rereleased uncut with a 15 certificate. Maybe it was because it was directed by Tobe Hooper that the DPP took against it.
Status: Available uncut.

THE GESTAPO'S LAST ORGY (1977)

A young woman is taken to a special female-only prisoner of war camp by the Nazis, and is forced to pleasure and amuse the German troops who pass through. The women are experimented on and abused in a film with little of artistic merit but a lot of exploitation value for collectors.

Status: Not currently on release in the UK.

THE HOUSE BY THE CEMETERY (1981)

The DPP really didn't get on with Lucio Fulci's horror output, did they? This glorious film formed the last part of his rather gothic undead/Gates Of Hell trilogy (the other parts being *The City Of The Living Dead* and *The Beyond*), and until its rather ambiguous ending (which could also be argued that Fulci just didn't know how to end it), it is one of the maestro's most coherent and consistent movies.

People are disappearing under grisly circumstances in order to be experimented on/harvested by the sinister and horrifically-visaged Dr. Freudstein. Essentially an Italian knockoff of the Frankenstein concept, the film starred Catriona MacColl and Paolo Malco in roles that would lift the film up into a higher echelon with their talents. While not as gory as his other horror films of the same era, *The House By The Cemetery* has a great atmosphere, almost akin to a nightmarish Hammer movie which has slipped into utterly demented territory.

An exquisite film, but due to some of the more shocking kills featured in it (A knife through the head, which sticks out of the victim's mouth, for example!), it was destined to fall foul of the editing room and the DPP's overzealous rampage across the video shelves.

Status: Now available fully uncut.

HOUSE ON THE EDGE OF THE PARK (1980)

After the controversy and social uproar that followed Wes Craven's *Last House On The Left*, you'd have thought its star,

David Hess, would have wanted to go in a different direction. Instead he returned in what is arguably an even more unsettling film from *Cannibal Holocaust* maestro Ruggero Deodato. Two criminals crash a house party, leading to an orgy of rape and violence with a wonderfully conceived ending. Tension is high and performances are good throughout. Uneasy viewing, but stylish and compelling. Incidentally, if you check out the trailer on YouTube, you may well notice the title has been composited incorrectly onscreen, instead reading *'The House On The Park Of The Edge'*.
Status: Available almost uncut

HUMAN EXPERIMENTS (1979)
A women-in-prison exploitation movie in which an innocent country singer finds herself being experimented on by a prison psychiatrist. Very 70s and a little unnerving, but the atrocious acting stops the viewer being able to take it seriously. Cheap and nasty. Not great, but not the worst of the bunch.
Status: No UK rerelease.

I MISS YOU, HUGS & KISSES (1978)
Also known as *Drop Dead Dearest*, this shoddy, woefully cheap and poorly executed (no pun intended) film is based on a real Canadian murder case. It was shoved on the DPP's list due to scenes where a corpse is fondled and for some shots of a woman being clubbed over he head. Or possibly just because it was a rubbish film. Either's possible.
Status: No UK rerelease since the cut version in 1986.

I SPIT ON YOUR GRAVE (1978)
Also known as *Day of the Woman*. One of the most famous of all of the Video Nasties (mainly thanks to the infamous cover featuring a model - allegedly a teenaged Demi Moore - baring her backside while clutching a bloody knife, surrounded by a lurid yellow frame), *I Spit On Your Grave* is the archetypal revenge movie.

Camille Keaton plays the lead, a girl who goes for a break in the country who ends up beaten and raped by a gang of hooligans, and after being left for dead she tracks them all own and slaughters them one by one in increasingly vile ways. Impossible to class as entertainment, the movie s more a gruelling exercise on endurance. It's hard to watch, but even harder to look away from. Disgusting, but formidable.

Status: Available in many cuts, none of them uncut in the UK.

INFERNO (1980)

The second part of Dario Argento's Three Mothers trilogy (the other parts being 1977's *Suspiria* and 2007's *Mother of Tears*), Inferno is a masterpiece of surreal supernatural horror art. Beautifully shot and directed, the film loses a bit of power thanks to some shoddy performances here and there, but it continues the art-horror giallo feel of *Suspiria* in fine style if not to the same level of madness and cinematic poetry.

I'm not entirely sure why it was seen as 'obscene' by the lunatics in power at the time, as it's really not very extreme. Unsettling, dreamlike and occasionally totally incomprehensible it may be, but obscene it certainly isn't. *Inferno*'s legendary underwater ballroom scene is nightmarish, but nothing in the film strays into out and out gore or exploitation. It's a murder mystery, an urban gothic tale, a supernatural horror movie and quite frankly, a work of art.

Status: Available uncut

ISLAND OF DEATH (1976)

Here's a film that really does deserve its place on the nasties list. At points it goes too far even for my tastes. A brother and sister with murderous and incestuous inclinations go on a tour of a Greek Island and wreak havoc across it, killing and screwing everything in sight. Including a goat. Notorious for its extremities of violence and sex rather than its quality, *Island of Death* isn't really an enjoyable film experience. One for completists and sadists more than general film fans. At one point a release on video was attempted under the title *Psychic Killer II*, although it has nothing to do with that vastly superior film, and not a psychic in sight! Nonsense.

Status: Now available uncut.

THE KILLER NUN (1978)

Blaxploitation, Nazisploitation and Nunsploitation. The Video Nasties list was rife with stuff that was intended to shock and titillate, and this shady film from Giulio Berruti does both of those things for its fans. The plot is in the title, really. Add a massive amount of needless flesh on display and sexualised violence and you have the recipe for a flick just begging to be attacked by censors.

Status: Now available uncut.

THE LAST HOUSE ON THE LEFT (1972)

Wes Craven's brutal and uncompromising directorial debut horrified audiences around the world with its raw and unsettling depictions of rape and extreme violence. A gang of brash thugs terrorize, beat, sexually assault and finally murder innocent girls... And then their father finds out, and the film gets REALLY nasty.

This film was the origin of the tag line *'To avoid fainting, keep repeating: It's only a movie... Only a movie... Only a movie.'* David Hess leads his thugs on their rampage, a role which garnered him the love and respect f genre and exploitation movie fans around the world for decades until his untimely death. As nasty and upsetting as this film is, *The Last House On The Left* is an extremely well structured piece of cinematic shock and suspense, as well as featuring some truly disturbing violence.

Status: Now available uncut

LATE NIGHT TRAINS (1975)

Also known as *Night Train Murders*, this unsettling film is basically along the lines of *The Last House On The Left* and

House At The Edge Of The Park, but set on a train. Hoodlums take a bunch of travellers prisoner and humiliate, torture and murder their way through the running time. Low on horror content, it is nevertheless high on uncomfortable viewing. Very, very tense at points. Definitely morally questionable, even to a gorehound like me.
Status: Now available uncut in the UK.

THE LIVING DEAD AT THE MANCHESTER MORGUE (1974)

Released under more titles than I've had BBQ chicken wings (i.e. roughly a bajillion, including *Let Sleeping Corpses Lie* and *Don't Open The Window*), this is one of the better movies of the zombie era, with some startling cinematography and a strong sense of atmosphere.

Shot mainly in Italy but with much of the countryside footage shot in England, this Anglo-Spanish-Italian co-production tells a tale of zombies attacking all and sundry after being awakened by an agricultural device which uses sonar waves to promote crop growth. There's an environmental message to the film, but mainly the viewer is interested in watching people being eviscerated by flesh-hungry corpses.

Definitely inspired stylistically by Romero's immortal *Night Of The Living Dead*, the film follows a biker played by Ray Lovelock and a girl played by Cristina Galbo, who are flung together as an unwitting hero and heroine after a vehicle accident. The two of them become swift friends and reluctant zombie fighters once the Yorkshire countryside is awash with recently risen bodies.

Speaking of which, there are a couple of zombies in *The Living Dead At The Manchester Morgue* which are truly iconic and extremely memorable, namely the bearded fellow we meet early on and the morgue zombie with a bandaged head and a massive autopsy scar. The latter is truly chilling during the morgue scenes, mainly thanks down to the strange and understated makeup. These aren't bright blue zombies like *Dawn of the Dead*, or like Fulci's porridge-faced ghouls, but rather they still resemble living people, albeit paler. And cannibalistic.

One aspect in which the film is ahead of others of the era is that the lead characters are pretty believable, and as such you do find yourself rooting for them. Especially Lovelock's roguish biker character. An absolute essential.
Status: Available uncut.

LOVE CAMP 7 (1969)
Two female British officers enter a secret Nazi stronghold in order to quiz - and possibly rescue - one of the inmates. What they discover is the typical tale of depravity, experimentation, torture and gratuitous nudity that the nazisploitation genre is known for, however, this one got their first, and essentially created the genre. In fact, this one possibly has more nudity in it than any of the others. A one-handed viewing session, if that's your thing.
Status: Not available uncut in the UK.

MADHOUSE (1981)
Also known as *There Was A Little Girl, Madhouse* is basically a gory thriller with elements stolen from various genre classics such as *Psycho* and *The Omen*. An incoherent script stops the film dead in its tracks at many points, but there's enough blood and nastiness to keep the fiends out there happy.
Status: Available uncut.

MARDI GRAS MASSACRE (1978)
A guy in a welder's mask butchers a number of prostitutes in this semi-remake of the Herschell Gordon Lewis splatter classic *Blood Feast* from 1963, and thus it pretty much does what the title says it will do. One particularly grisly scene has our masked villain indulge in genital mutilation and amputation with an early victim. Not an easy watch, but one of the more rare tapes in the list.
Status: Never resubmitted for classification.

NIGHT OF THE BLOODY APES (1979)
There's actually only one 'ape' in the movie, namely a shirtless guy with atrocious monster makeup wandering around killing people following a experiment gone awry. This curious little film found its way into the nasties list due to the stock footage of open heart surgery rather than the somewhat comical violence. You're not missing much by not seeing this one.

Status: Unavailable uncut.

NIGHT OF THE DEMON (1980)
This surreal film about an anthropology class searching for the Sasquatch is an odd watch. Somewhat disjointed in terms of narrative and direction, it does nonetheless have a mutant baby and a guy getting his penis torn off. I addition there is a fair amount of other dismemberment (as it were) on offer, but the constant flashbacks and mish-mash of styles leaves a lot of viewers wondering what it was that they just sat through. It does, however, retain a cut following.
Status: Available with some cuts.

NIGHTMARE MAKER (1982)
One of my 'holy grail' VHS tapes – which I still don't own a copy of – I've always had a fascination with this particular Video Nasty for a bit of an odd reason. You see, Nightmare Maker (also known as *Butcher, Baker, Nightmare Maker* and *Night Warning)* showed up in an episode of one of the greatest British comedy shows of the 1980s – *The Young Ones*.

   The episode was called "Nasty" and centred around the misfits in the Young Ones house trying to figure out how to work a VCR. The tape is visible in various shots, and to me that grounds it in the era even more than the Video Nasties controversy itself, making it hugely desirable to a sad, twisted individual like me. That episode of *The Young Ones* also featured The Damned performing their cult smash "Nasty", a song which sums the feel of the era up perfectly for me. Check it out.

The film itself is an interesting curio, harrowing and horrific and deserving of its Video Nasties status when you consider the attitudes of the era. A man is framed for murder when he is suspected of a gay love triangle by a bigot, but the truth about the murderer is even more creepy. Incest, brutal murders, stylish direction and some pretty decent performances raise *Nightmare Maker* up from being standard slasher fare and into something almost art-house. Very different from the rest of the pack.
Status: Not currently available uncut in the UK.

NIGHTMARES IN A DAMAGED BRAIN (1981)

This film from director Romano Scavolini is one of the most sought-after of all of the Video Nasties tapes, and not just because of the chilling scenes of murder and madness and hideous gore, but also because in its raw and uncut form it is at times an astonishingly well-made psychological thriller. Some people may disagree with me on that score, but I do maintain that *Nightmares In A Damaged Brain* is a damn good movie as well as being a damn good horror movie.

It went down in history due to its distributor being jailed after refusing to edit out a piece of footage lasting exactly one second. That alone demonstrates the extent of the mania surrounding these films and their supposed influence over the public that a single second of film can get someone locked up just because of its potential power over viewers. That's fascinating, and more than a little bit scary too.

The film follows a troubled man suffering flashbacks to a violent childhood episode which cause him to go on a killing spree while wearing a chilling mask of an old man's face. The film carries some genuine shocks and some stylish cinematography, and is rather more than just the straightforward slasher/exploitation movie that some would have you believe it to be. Occasionally nonsensical it may be, but *Nightmares In A Damaged Brain* (aka just *NIGHTMARE* in the US) remains a powerful viewing experience to this day for many lovers of the Video Nasties era.

Status: Not currently available uncut in the UK.

POSSESSION (1981)
This French-made psychological thriller is beautifully made, although at points hard to follow. Starring Sam Neill and Isabelle Adjani, *Possession* is one of the most artistic of all the films on the Video Nasties list. Aside from a shocking ending involving a very strange (and very messy) creature, the film features little that would really deem it to be particularly 'nasty' aside from some scenes of self-harm and a lot of overacting. A fine film, but not one for diehard horror addicts. That said, the VHS editions of this tend to have some amazing artwork.
Status: Available uncut.

PRANKS (1982)
Also known as *The Dorm That Dripped Blood* and *Death Dorm*, this movie has to be seen in its uncut form or it comes across as a standard slasher movie with not a lot to to set it apart from the rest of the pack. If you watch the full version of the film though, it has more bite to it and provides a better overall experience. That said, doesn't that go for all of the films in the list? A group of college kids stay at a dorm over Christmas before the place is demolished and find themselves being offed by an unknown maniac. Good, wholesome fun.
Status: Available with 10 seconds cut.

PRISONER OF THE CANNIBAL GOD (1978)
Perhaps better known in some places as *Mountain Of The Cannibal God*, this uneven and somewhat slow movie stars Bond girl Ursula Andress on the trail of her missing adventurer husband. Naturally, her journey into the jungle ends up with her and her cohorts falling foul of a cannibal tribe. Cue nudity, gore, needless animal cruelty, stock footage and some exploited locals.
Status: Available with 2 minutes of cuts.

REVENGE OF THE BOGEY MAN (1983)

A poor sequel to the original movie written about further up the list, this cheap cash-in consists mainly of flashbacks to the first film, a few new scenes and a flimsy plot attempting to hold it all together. Watchable, but only if you gave a decent attention span. And heck, if you've seen the first one then you've already seen 40 minutes of this one too!
Status: Available in a recut version.

THE SLAYER (1982)
A group of people are stranded on a strange island, and one of their number has been suffering prophetic and at times gory nightmares since childhood, nightmares which suggest that this island is where the beast in her dreams lives. Could the killings she envisions be coming true? It's sometimes hard to tell what's real and what isn't in this stylish yet slow-paced chiller. There are some decent quality effects sequences which do have an impact when they finally arrive, and a cast which is just about passable. If you can stand the slow pace, then you may well find something of an atmospheric gem in *The Slayer*.
Status: Now available uncut.

SNUFF (1974)
This is an interesting one, but mainly for the gall and ingenuity of the people involved. The people behind the release bought a failed South American exploitation movie, retitled it and added an extra five minutes at the end. It's that extra footage which put the film on the DPP's list, as it depicted the moments after 'Cut' had been called on the film itself and the crew turn on a young lady from the cast and brutally murder her in front of the cameras. Of course, it's completely fake and unconvincing, but the idea had the desired effect and brought audiences to the film to see what the fuss was about. Naturally, it was banned outright.
Status: Not currently available in the UK.

SS EXPERIMENT CAMP (1976)
One of the most notorious of all of the Nazisploitation movies, *SS Experiment Camp* fell into the DPP's trap pretty much as soon

as the videos hit the shelves thanks to the artwork, depicting a naked woman crucified upside-down. Some knickers were painted over her modesty to try and soften the image a bit, but how can you soften the image of a crucified naked woman at all? It doesn't work like that. The film itself concerns the usual sort of human experiments and humiliation which are de rigeur with the sub-genre, but for all of the violence, nudity, occasional gore scenes and atrociously bad taste, the film is actually pretty well shot. And yeah, the shot on the cover does show up in it. Not one to watch with the parents, though!
Status: Available uncut. I'm actually kinda surprised.

TENEBRAE (1982)

Dario Argento's giallo masterpiece, this fell foul of the censors and authorities due to some very graphic gore and misogynistic violence. Very elegantly made, it is at heart a whodunnit, albeit one with blood spraying artfully in all directions, severed arms and suchlike liberally flung at the screen. A thriller in most aspects, it nevertheless has a horror movie atmosphere and absolutely bags of tension. One of the finest examples of the giallo genre, and an absolute must-see for any horror or thriller fan. Yes, it's dated now, but it remains a brilliant and beautifully composed piece of filmmaking.
Status: Now available uncut in the UK.

TERROR EYES (1981)

Also known elsewhere as *Night School*, this slasher movie features a selection of murders by decapitation amongst a group of college coeds. I mean, what else went on in American colleges in that era other than shagging, weed and murder? The killer is dressed simply in motorbike leathers and a helmet, and while the killings are pretty nasty, there's nothing grotesque or offensive enough to warrant any concern over it corrupting the public. Another case of 'How did this end up on the list?'
Status: Available with small cuts.

THE TOOLBOX MURDERS (1978)

This movie is one of the films that you can indeed understand why the BBFC went mental when they saw it. Mind you, that may be down to the BBFC types of the age being repressed and uncomfortable with their own sense of identity rather than the amount of 70s pubic hair on display, or indeed the several brutal murders. A masked man is going around the city with a selection of power tools, hammers, saws and more for his spree of butchery. Essentially a murder mystery thriller with more blood and more flesh than usual, the film takes a harrowing turn at the halfway point and then really starts to screw with your expectations. Dark rather than kitsch, the film retains a lot of its shock power when viewed today. Just whatever you do, don't see the bloody terrible remake.
Status: Available with minimal cuts.

UNHINGED (1982)
As a horror movie, *Unhinged* doesn't really deliver the goods until its ending, when it does bring on the red stuff. As a film in general it's a downbeat and somewhat bleak flick which doesn't offer what a lot of people want from a Video Nasty. Three girls are on their way to a jazz festival (yeah right...) when their car plunges into a ravine during a storm. The girls awaken in a creepy mansion populated by creepy people, and then... not much happens until the last five minutes. You kinda have to be in the mood for this one, as if you're looking for thrills and gore galore, then you've picked up the wrong tape. The ending's pretty solid though.
Status: Available uncut.

VISITING HOURS (1982)
Michael Ironside and William Shatner in a Video Nasty? Yup, two people with genuinely impressive pedigrees in film and TV wound up in a slasher movie which hit the DPP's list. Set in a hospital, there are a few shades of Halloween II, but only because of the setting. The setting actually makes it a bit different to a lot of other more standard slashers, and the cast helps to give it some gravitas too, even though it's a pretty standard stalk-and-slash

movie. Another example of a film which doesn't really belong on the list as it's not as graphic as the authorities of the 1980s would have you believe.
Status: Available with 1 minute of cuts.

THE WEREWOLF AND THE YETI (1975)
This Spanish movie, original title *La Maldicion de la Bestia* (*Curse of the Beast*), is actually the eighth in a series about the titular lycanthrope, and plays exactly like the z-grade cheapie you would imagine it to be. And yes, the Werewolf and the Yeti do indeed battle it out. Nudity and gore abound, but both are tame by today's standards. Strangely, this one didn't even get a UK release, let alone a rerelease!
Status: Not available in the UK.

THE WITCH WHO CAME FROM THE SEA (1976)
This American movie is one of the most sought after Video Nasties for a good number of VHS collectors, and while it's never really held me under its spell (if you'll excuse the term), I can completely see the appeal. Here's a film with a weird title, often seen with garish and eye-catching artwork, and a film within the case which is completely different to what you may expect from the title and advertising. Essentially a twisted psychological fable about a woman trying to deal with sexual abuse by abusing men back, it is an uncomfortable and at times truly shocking look into the broken psyche of the main character. A film for the more esoteric moments rather than a gore party.
Status: Available uncut.

WOMEN BEHIND BARS (1975)
Directed by the late, great Jess Franco (under a pseudonym), this exploitation movie follows a gangster's moll into prison after murdering her man, and her subsequent torture and grim life behind bars in a prison stuffed with angry women. It's a Franco movie, so there's a fair bit of flesh, which is probably what landed it on the Video Nasties list more than the limited violence on show. Having said that, there's a scene of genital torture which definitely had something to do with it.

Status: Not currently available in the UK.

ZOMBIE CREEPING FLESH (1980)
Also known as *Virus, Hell of The Living Dead* and other titles, this ridiculously cheesy zombie chomp-fest is something of a mess, as it basically feels like two films cut together. In fact, that's pretty much how it was made, as the direction of Bruno Mattei was added to by screenwriter Claudio Fragrasso, and the two styles are very clear in their differences. A group of commandos are sent to the jungle to wipe out some terrorists, but their efforts are made even harder when they come under attack from the living dead, supposedly reanimated by a secret virus that has escaped from a laboratory. The film looks (and certainly is) cheap, but there are some tense standoff scenes and some enjoyable zombie carnage to be witnessed. Not one of the greatest zombie films ever, but not the worst of the bunch from that era.
Status: Available uncut.

ZOMBIE FLESH EATERS (1979)
And so the alphabetical end to the DPP's list of Video Nasties movies brings us one of the greatest horror movies ever made, and you're welcome to debate that statement all you want. *Zombie Flesh Eaters* is the apex of the Italian zombie movie era, and while that may not say much to some people, to geeks like us it says a heck of a lot. Directed by the late lunatic genius that was Lucio Fulci (he of *The Beyond* and *House By The Cemetery* from earlier in the DPP's list), it perfectly sums up the genre as well as pushes it to an extreme.

Packed with now-legendary moments such as a zombie wrestling a shark, the close-ups of the worm-infested zombies themselves, the fat guy zombie emerging from the boat or THAT final shot over the bridge, *Zombie Flesh Eaters* is one of the minority of Video Nasties titles that you can return to again and again and still enjoy. Beautifully shot (even the legendary 'eye gouged out with splintered wood' scene is well-executed) with vividly exotic locations and brutally visceral splatter, it remains one of the most beloved zombie movies of all time, right up there with genuine genre classics like *Dawn of the Dead*.

Speaking of which, *Zombie Flesh Eaters* was billed as sort-of an unofficial sequel to George A. Romero's follow-up to *Night Of The Living Dead*, going as far as being entitled *ZOMBIE 2* (DOTD's original title was *ZOMBIE* in some places) for a while. It's not a follow-up, of course. I like to think of it as its own entity (and I try to forget about the sequels which followed in its wake), such is the quality of the movie itself. Fulci films are generally known to be somewhat patchy affairs, but *Zombie Flesh Eaters* is one where he got a massive amount of it right. It still suffers from the usual Italian thing of dubbing actors in after the film has been shot, so a lot of the dialogue sounds really fake, but the performances of people like Tisa Farrow, Ian McCullloch, Al Cliver, Richard Johnson and others ensure that the hokey nonsense onscreen rings true at least to itself.

The power of *Zombie Flesh Eaters* isn't with the script though. That power is almost entirely visual, with shots and ideas the likes of which the viewing public had never seen before. The camera didn't turn away from even the most gruesome and blood-soaked frames, the zombies were chilling despite their cheap makeup and the score by Fabio Frizzi and others is just a monumental piece of work.

There is a sense of claustrophobia to the most intense scenes of the film, a tension which helps to maintain your suspension of disbelief until the next gut-munching, blood-spraying shot hits you.

Up there with *Cannibal Holocaust, The Driller Killer* and *I Spit On Your Grave, Zombie Flesh Eaters* was basically asking for trouble from the Conservative government at the time.

Actually, none of them were asking for trouble at all. They were just films. Just video tapes. They didn't corrupt people. They entertained them.

Speaking of the Video Nasties, you really must check out the following release as soon as you possibly can.

Andrew Hawnt

VIDEO NASTIES: THE BEST BOX SET EVER?

When I saw this beast of a box set go on sale, I knew that I would have to very quickly become intimately acquainted with it. Erm, not like that, you filthy minded little gnome. *Video Nasties: The Definitive Guide* really is the genuine article – an incredible feature-length documentary (*VIDEO NASTIES: MORAL PANIC, CENSORSHIP AND VIDEOTAPE*), rare trailers for all 72 titles (with fascinating intro pieces), company idents and more. This mammoth set has a total running time of *13 and a half hours* and is gripping throughout. I cannot recommend this box set highly enough, and while it was produced in a somewhat limited run, there are still copies to be found quite easily in all the usual places online. It wasn't cheap when it first came out, but it was worth every penny as it's genuinely a brilliant piece of work throughout.

Directed by Jake West (director of many other projects, including the movies *Doghouse, Pumpkinhead: Ashes To Ashes, Evil Aliens* and the notorious *Razor Blade Smile*), the documentary uses new interviews and archive footage to maximum effect, creating what is essentially a perfect time capsule and a pretty much perfect overview of the Video Nasties era and societal influence. For those that weren't aware or alive at the time of the whole scandal, it is a fascinating piece of work which shows just how far the controversy stretched.

People were arrested, businesses ruined, countless tapes flung into furnaces, and the Video Nasties films themselves essentially blamed for the downfall of civilization. Rape, murders, assaults and all manner of other real world horrors were blamed directly on Video Nasties. The documentary is a perfect evaluation of that demented hysteria and the films that found themselves on the DPP's list. And the rest of the material in the set is sublime as well. Find it, buy it and enjoy every damn second.

IT'S POSSIBLE TO BE SOCIAL AND A VHS FAN

That's not meant to sound patronizing. I have first-hand experience that the practice of being a VHS enthusiast doesn't mean you're limited to spending your nights alone in a dark room with no company other than a stack of tapes and a VCR you're always worried is about to finally fail after decades of service. I've had some fabulous nights with friends involving VHS tapes and associated films of the era, and that's not in the dirty sense, you filthy minded animal.

Years ago I used to go to a regular *Doctor Who* night which I helped to devise. A bunch of old-school *Doctor Who* fans like myself would gather, along with our respective partners in some cases, for an evening watching and discussing the greatest science fiction show in history, eating bowls of show-centric Jelly Babies, drinking tea (and other more powerful liquids) and generally having a great old time being as geeky as possible. Granted, those nights also included DVDs of the new era episodes, but for the most part it was all about the VHS tapes, that tactile link to much-missed eras of our own lives.

More recently I went to a cinema event at the Broadway Cinema here in Nottingham to an event dubbed *THE ALL NIGHT BAD MOVIE EXPERIENCE*, and what a spectacular night it was. The four films were the notorious amateur drama *The Room*, 1980s action cheese-fest *Samurai Cop* (you really can't go wrong with Robert Z'dar as a bad guy), Patrick Swayze's *Road House* (hardly a bad film if you think about it), and classic slasher movie *Pieces*. The films were shown back to back, along with classic trailers between each one. Three of the four films were shown from vintage 35mm prints, as were the trailers. About 150 people were there with me, heckling and cheering throughout the night as each film unfolded and the crowd got more drunk. By the end of the event it was 8am, light outside and the cinema auditorium looked like a war zone of empty beer cans, Red Bull cans and snack boxes. I went back home and collapsed into bed, my senses fried from nine hours of retro movie fun with like minded film idiots. The night was a genius idea and I would go to another event in a heartbeat.

Even more recently I staged a movie double-bill at the Broadway Cinema for my Stag night before getting married the following month. I wanted mayhem, and while I couldn't play VHS on the big screen, I did screen a double helping of *Street Trash* and *Class of Nuke 'Em High*, which was a dream come true, sat there watching trashy movies with my friends before heading to the famous Annie's Burger Shack for beer and ludicrous food.

There is an appetite out there for film lovers to see classic and not-so-classic films on the big screen, or at least in a public setting.

A perfect example is the *STRAIGHT TO VIDEO* movie nights at the independent SCREEN 22 cinema. At those nights, classics from the video era are brought back to a cinema screen, fans are urged to dress up, and there are even occasional giveaways, all in the confines of a little indie cinema which understands it's audience and how to put on a great night (you can find an interview with Rob Lane from the *Straight To Video* night and its associated music project elsewhere in this book). It was at one of these events I first saw the glorious VHS collector documentary *Adjust Your Tracking*.

These social ideas for enjoying cult films from the VHS era should be encouraged, as there are thousands of films that deserve a showing, and a sea of film lovers who want entertainment that truly appeals to them. One day I would love to own a little place and screen some films, or at least run a vintage horror night somewhere. Although, what to watch first? The eternal film geek problem.

LAPSING FROM HORROR

As with a lot of horror VHS fans, horror hasn't been the only genre which has held my attention over the years. In fact, there was a time where I had literally no horror whatsoever in my cinematic diet. That was a period in which I had discovered something else entirely, namely the world of low budget action/sci-fi/martial arts b-movies. The straight-to-video delights those genres gave me when I needed them the most were a shot of adrenaline after feeling like I was watching nothing but the same horror film over and again with different titles (an ailment any genre-specific collector/viewer can surely relate to).

I discovered a universe of movie heroes I'd never really been exposed to, apart from the goddess of martial arts capers, Cynthia Rothrock. There guys like Olivier Gruner and Gary Daniels kicking ass in films like *Nemesis* and *Fist Of The North Star*, and companies like PM Entertainment, Trimark Pictures, Imperial Entertainment and Green Communications.

Films that caught my eye during that time included things like Project *Shadowchaser* and its million sequels, *A.P.E.X, Evolver, T-Force, The Digital Man,* the aforementioned *Arcade* and many others. Hell, I even sat through the sort-of-unofficial straight-to-video *Universal Soldier* sequels. I got through a hell of a lot of martial arts movies and action flicks starring people like Robert Ginty or Rutger Hauer, just for the sheer fun they presented, as well as the lack of brain cells needed to enjoy them.

To me the beauty of these films was the fact that so much scale was attempted on such tiny budgets, which varying results. Even when those efforts failed spectacularly, you had to respect the fact they'd at least tried. I mean, it's easy for filmmakers to cut away or to refer to something in dialogue rather than show it onscreen when the money's tight, but there's a lot to be said for crews doing what they can to get a more epic vision onscreen.

Case in point would be the action/Sci-fi mini-epic *A.P.E.X,* about a science guy who screws up history so much that the present he returns to is drastically different, a world in which he must join up with a team of battle-hardened soldiers in an endless war against robotic invaders from across time. Yeah, that sound amazing, doesn't it?

Well the robots look like what they are – rubber suits with a daft shaped head, and the computer generated time travel effects look suspiciously like an early 1990s computer screensaver, but come on, they tried! There were some great ideas in that film, and the cast played it just the right side of cheesy, making it a huge amount of fun for an impressionable mind like mine. In fact, my love for that stuff went so far at one point that I started writing scripts to try and pitch to the companies who made those films. Some kids dream of making big budget blockbusters stuffed with state of the art effects and real actors, while I always wanted to make cheap crap with people you've never heard of and special effects that look like they were created with crayons and a bit of string.

For a while, I was addicted to Ninjas. Any video tape I could find that hd a ninja on it was treasure to me. This ended up with me discovering a hell of a lot of shitty films, but also some unintentionally hilarious gems. Stuff like *Ninja Warrior, Ninja Kids: Kiss of Death* and the TV-shows-cut-into-makeshift-movies *American Commando Ninja* (which had no Americans or commandos in it) and its sequel *Born A Ninja* was gold to me, a weird window into a world I didn't understand and could barely follow the plots of (mainly down to some truly hilarious attempts at dubbing). The main perpetrator in demented ninja movies was Joseph Lai and his IFD ARTS company. Those guys bought up a load of failed Chinese and Japanese action/crime movies and spliced them with gloriously bad new footage of white guys in colourful ninja costumes having superhero-style fights. Films like *Ninja Hunt, Ninja The Protector, Golden Ninja Warrior, The Ninja Squad* and something like 35 other titles came out under that regime, all of them utterly mental and deliciously rubbish. Hell, the label even spawned a horror movie entitled Scorpion Thunderbolt, which was a failed horror movie intercut with more new footage and retitled. That was so very mad that it's almost impossible to follow (and thus well-worth a look).

In the days when horror wasn't my focal point, tapes of TV series, making-of videos for movies, music video collections and all kinds of other crap found its way onto my shelves. However, it would always be horror that I would come back to. Sometimes you just want to sit back with a good slasher movie or a film about giant alien penises with teeth (*The Deadly Spawn* – check it out!), and that kind thing has never lost its appeal to me. Erm I mean the films, not giant alien cocks.

HORROR MOVIE REMAKES

Actually, something which is even worse than a lot of old-school VHS flicks is the recent slew of horror movie remakes, which have taken truly iconic, genre-defining films which have enthralled people for decades and turned them into cheap and quick ripoffs.

Let's do a quick headcount of horror films from the VHS era which have been remade for a new audience and royally screwed up: *A Nightmare On Elm Street, Friday the 13th, Halloween, Halloween 2, The Hills Have Eyes, The Hills Have Eyes 2, Last House On The Left, The Texas Chainsaw Massacre* (which even got a lousy prequel and then ANOTHER remake), *Night Of The Demons, Night Of The Living Dead, Dawn Of The Dead, Day Of The Dead, The Hitcher, The Crazies, Invasion Of The Body Snatchers, The Toolbox Murders, The Omen, Let The Right One In* (Remade as *Let Me In*), *My Bloody Valentine, Sorority Row, The Thing, The Amityville Horror, Carnival Of Souls, The Fog, The Haunting, House Of Wax, House On Haunted Hill, I Spit On Your Grave, The Wicker Man, [REC]* (remade as *QUARANTINE*), *Carrie, Maniac* and many more.

And many, many more to come.

It sickens me that these classic titles are brought out to a new generation as watered-down copies, rather than new editions of the originals. As far as I see it, studios should just take the original films, clean up the prints, beef up the soundtracks and retouch the special effects, giving audiences a new look at the real thing.

This would be cheaper for studios and more effective, gaining more revenue from existing titles and broadening the horizons of contemporary film fans who haven't been exposed to the films which shaped the medium. Remakes cheapen the genre, they cheapen what made it great in the first place and they cheapen an industry which thrilled and enthralled the world for years.

But what do I know? I'm just a guy who loves films, many of which are so bad that it's almost impossible for other people to understand the appeal, a guy who grew up gazing at posters and magazines and VHS covers and found magic in the films they brought me. A guy who thinks that Hollywood should make something new. Something unique. Not making the same damn thing over and over again with ever diminishing returns. There is a world absolutely teeming with new, raw talent which is begging to be tapped. Chances aren't being taken with these endless remakes, and while chances aren't being taken, opportunities are being missed.

These remakes are not completely without merit, though. The people who work on them all have a great deal of talent, but it's such a shame that their talents are being wasted on remakes with such a brief shelf-life. After the initial rush of interest in a remade film, people will tend to go back to the original and revisit that far more often than the remake. Take the newest version of *A Nightmare On Elm Street*, for example (people have already forgotten about it!). That terrible remake only served to strengthen the belief that Wes Craven's original was so brilliant. Jackie Earle Hayley was a great choice for Freddy Krueger, but the makeup he was hidden under looked ridiculous. Robert Englund's legendary Freddy makeup (created originally by Kevin Yagher) may not have been medically accurate, but it worked for the character, and after all, I've always seen Freddy's dream demon self as more of a representation of the character's evil, rather than a literal image of what he'd look like burned. I mean, he still has clothes and so on, so it's not that close to reality in the first place, is it?

Remakes will never be able to top the real thing. By their very definition they lack originality, and even when a film takes a different direction to what came before, it will always be compared – usually unfavourably – with the real thing.

Give it a rest, Hollywood.

THRILLER VIDEO:
ABOUT AS COOL AS IT GETS

As a UK collector, I've never really been exposed all that much to US releases of movies, but in recent years as a devoted old school VHS collector I have heard and seen a great deal about the famous Thriller Video releases, which sound like the coolest things ever. Why do they appeal so much? Basically because they were largely awful movies presented at either end by the glorious presence of Elvira, Mistress of the Dark.

If you're not familiar with the creation of comedian Cassandra Peterson, then I'd have to question our friendship, but in a nutshell she created a kitsch and corny horror hostess with a beehive and a delightfully cheesy costume who would crack bad jokes and essentially take the piss out of the films she was hosting. I've seen clips on YouTube of these delights and would love to collect them. However, even though I have a beautiful and ancient VCR which can play NTSC as well as PAL tapes, I don't have the cash to lay out to get hold of those amazing looking tapes.

The artwork for each one is brilliant, with Elvira posing in a suitably cheesecake fashion beside the gaudy poster art for the movie held within. Elvira has always been a cool character in my eyes, sarcastic, acerbic and downright hilarious at times, and far from just being a glamourous hostess with a famous chest. Peterson came up with a great character which is genuinely funny, and couple that with cheap horror and science fiction movies (or in some cases TV episodes) and it sounds like VHS paradise to me.

I think Thriller video is something I shall have to admire from afar due to my piss-poor finances, but that won't stop me giving a shout out to the awesome collectors around the world who have managed to get hold of these things. The big box art for them is superb, and the delights within just sound perfect to me.

Not all of the Thriller Video releases featured Elvira hosting them and her image on the packaging (such as the infamous release of *Make Them Die Slowly* – aka *Cannibal Ferox*), and once her involvement ended, interest in the range dried up. Still, the Elvira-fronted Thriller Videos are a delight to check out and fascinating to research. Why odd we get nothing that cool over here? What did we get? the BBFC ruining every horror movie in sight and bloody Simon Mayo telling us a film might have "sexual swear words" in it.

Well, in light of that warning I'd say its a fucking travesty we didn't get those great releases over here, and if you're an American collector with them on your shelves, I am extremely jealous. Seriously, check their artwork and clips out and you'll understand just what a kitsch pleasure they are.

THE MADNESS OF VHS

Make no mistake about it, VHS tapes are able to house absolute insanity. As the video age made it far more possible for low budget films to make it out to audiences, VCR fans could get their fix of gore, action, sleaze and fun taken to a whole new level. Films like the notorious *Tales From The Quadead Zone* or the equally rare *Demon Queen* just wouldn't have been seen any other way. However, it's low and no-budget delights like those which often end up being more entertaining than hollow big budget fare.

VHS made it possible for us to see some of the weirdest, most obscure stuff ever filmed, and while not everything was an absolute classic, it was awesome to be able to check it out in the first place. Whatever your poison, VHS could get it rammed into your head via your ocular input devices (I mean your eyes. Sorry, there has been caffeine). Be it extreme horror, martial arts movies, screwball comedies, one-handed 'Erotic thrillers', science-fiction B/C/Z-movies, videos of old trains, car crashes, sports events, cartoons or a mixture of everything under the sun, the format was able to bring it into your home.

When video grew and became the norm across the planet, all manner of lunacy was made available to tape-hungry viewers, and that hunger for the weird, the strange and the extreme remains today in the current generation of VHS collectors. I mean, come on, you have to be a little bit screwed up in order to find entertainment value in stuff like Jorg Buttgereit's legendary *Nekromantik* necrophilia movies, or to search out a copy of *SNUFF* in order to check out the faked murder tagged onto the end of the film. Or demented kung-fu movies like the utter lunacy of *Master Of The Flying Guillotine* (seriously, check it out, but watch the trailer first to truly appreciate the full thing).

    Movies started to be shot on video too if the budget was small enough to make it necessary, and those shot-on-video (SOV to collectors) are often the most insane and entertaining of the, all, although not always intentionally. That is both the the beauty and the madness of the VHS format. Of course, a lot of this stuff can be found on DVD and occasionally even Blu-Ray, but neither of those formats have all that much heft for the fan of analogue media.

    Personally speaking I can't see future generations having the same nostalgic and sentimental connection to those soulless discs. It's a point I make over and over here, but it rings true every time. Digital media will never have the presence or the emotional attachment that analogue media brought to popular culture. It's the same for vinyl. For old video games. For 8-track tapes. Even laserdiscs have a nostalgic value for a lot of collectors, and while they were an early digital media, they still had the giant size and sense of ownership that came with vinyl.

    VHS was basically a way for the maniacs to be unleashed upon the people who wanted to indulge, and indulge we most certainly did. Of course, that explains why so many of us are a little bit odd. Or to put it another way: Lunatics who foam at the mouth whenever someone says "DVDs and Blu-Rays are so much better than VHS".

    Gah. Gragh.

    Grraaaarrrrggghh.

    BRRRAAAAAIIIINNNSSS!!!

HORROR VHS COLLECTORS ON FACEBOOK

Okay. Here's the big one. This chapter deals with one of the main reasons this book even exists, and that is a certain group on a certain social networking site. Hell, that group has even been the catalyst for a feature-length documentary.

There are moments when something seems so simple that you feel utterly stupid for not thinking of it yourself. Discovering a huge number of likeminded VHS horror collectors from across the world didn't happen through a ton of research or wandering endless message boards, but by just putting 'Horror VHS' into the search box on Facebook. Love it or hate it (I'm somewhere between the two), the big blue-and-white behemoth does provide bitter, obsessive geeks like me a place to connect with other bitter, obsessive geeks. Oh, and some genuinely brilliant people too. Mainly the former, though. The page I discovered is HORROR VHS COLLECTORS UNITE!

Founded by a gentleman, artist and devout collector named Earl Kess, the group has grown and evolved and mutated into something at once ugly and beautiful, addictive and annoying. I love it so much. The basic idea of the page is that members post photos of their latest purchases, be they found 'In The Wild' or bought online via eBay, Amazon or elsewhere.

The point? Simply to share enthusiasm for the format and the films which we love and want. There are posts offering sales and trades, queries and so on, and it's a most pleasant retreat from the daily drudgery of all those people in my life who don't share my addiction to a dead format and films which were largely not that great in terms of production values.

I've been a member of the page for quite some time now. Not from the beginning of the group, but certainly its early days. In that time the group has grown at an incredible rate and its current membership has now gone way past 5,000 VHS addicts. When I joined there was a mere 800. That's a lot of oddballs out there looking for old videos, and just the knowledge that I'm not the only one out there is remarkably reassuring. Of course, the page goes through times where people do nothing but argue to the point of basically inviting their opponents outside for a fistfight, but hey, that's how the internet was built, and it's all part of the page's charm.

Personally I try not to get involved with the in-fights, as I'm far more interested in peoples' tapes, memories and cool new finds. Naturally, the vast majority of the collectors in the group are based in the USA, but it was a breath of fresh air to find a few people on there from the UK, and it's been great getting to know those people a little better. Money changes hands for tapes on the group on a regular basis, and sometimes large amounts, but for the most part tapes go for a small price, or in the case of the guys I've met on there, we keep sending each other stuff for free just because we know who'll get a kick out of stuff we find.

My obsession with the group has become so bad that when I'm out looking for tapes and see something cool, my first thought isn't about the film itself or trying to make some cash off it, but rather "Oh man, the group are going to love this one." Yeah, almost two thousand people I've never met in real life have become some of the coolest people in the world to me.

One thing which is always fascinating about the group is seeing how the films differ from country to country, be it artwork, edits or packaging. I mean, I'm in the UK and as such rarely ever saw a slipcase VHS (although I did buy a few in the 1990s when they were dirt cheap, namely *Dawn of the Mummy*, *The Children Of Ravensback* and *Don't Go In The House* as well as a bunch of ninja movies like *Ninja Warrior, Ninja Kids: Kiss of Death* etc, which were even worse than the Joseph Lai cut-and-paste jobs), and our idea of a 'big box' VHS is to the guys in the States a large clamshell, while their big boxes are just that – big boxes which contain a container with the tape in it.

Then there are the collectors who keep posting tapes from Japan, or Denmark, or Mexico, countless films I've never heard of which look so deliciously trashy it beggars belief. These people are serious hardcore collectors, but that does sadly lead to cliques and alliances, as it does everywhere in the realm of collecting and cult geekery. That's how we're built. We have our opinions on stuff and we'll happily stay up far too late in order to argue a point.

Right now on there, giant arguments can erupt very quickly, soon filling the page with name-calling, the occasional threat of violence, or people being called-out for not paying for tapes or not sending tapes out that have been purchased by other collectors. This is utterly engrossing and addictive to witness. In an age where social media has become utterly mind-numbingly tedious, the Horror VHS Collectors Unite Facebook page continues to entertain and educate me from afar.

I haven't been able to post as much I used to in the group of late, due to the massive difference to my life since becoming a father and trying to juggle freelancing gigs and a dayjob with parenthood and occasionally a few seconds of restless sleep here and there. This is a shame to me as if you miss a few days then you kinda end up feeling a bit out of the loop with what everyone has been talking about and it can take a little while to get back into the swing of things.

There may be over five thousand members now but the group still seems to operate and thrive thanks to a central group of maybe 50-60 users. Sadly I wouldn't count myself amongst that core as I'm nowhere cool enough to stand alongside the heavy hitters of the group, plus I have nowhere near as much disposable income as I used to, meaning my VHS purchases have to be carefully executed these days. In addition, it's starting to become a difficult hobby to maintain as a UK collector. The price of tapes is going up thanks to a combination of nostalgia, financial gain, trends and even the occasional douche bidding tapes up intentionally to make a point that things are getting out of hand. I'll not mention who that was in these pages, as I don't want to start getting internet rage flung at me along with everything else I have to deal with on a daily basis.

Plus, I don't know the whole story. As with so much stuff on the web, not everything is as it seems, and while the practice of bidding tapes up just to make gullible people pay more for tapes and intentionally skewing the hobby is utterly reprehensible, I don't know all of the circumstances.

I did, however, read a fascinating and hilarious thread on the group about it.

You see, the group seems to have its own justice system, policed by the members themselves. If someone is wronged, duped out of cash, hasn't had their traded tapes delivered or is simply being harassed by another member, then the full might of hundreds of keyboards is unleashed and they are beaten into submission by private messages, tagged comments, Photoshopped spoof pictures and enough vitriol to make your spleen melt. These threads go from serious to potentially violent to hilariously entertaining within a few comments, and they can run for hours. Or days. Or weeks.

The true joy of the Horror VHS Collectors Unite! page is the fact that it exists at all. Yeah, VHS tapes have gained some notoriety again in recent times, but for the most part it is very much a niche hobby. Being able to interact with these people, collectors with both large scale and small scale collections, is such a gift. It's also nice to use Facebook for something other than pictures of my dinner or quiet cyber stalking of people I dislike.

The backbone of the group is the passion we all share for the format and the era of moviemaking which filled those tapes with such gaudy delights in the first place. The addiction I have to the group stems completely from the fact that so much stuff gets posted there. Granted, a lot of the time it's people trying to sell stuff, but those posts are still of interest as it gives us all a look at tapes we may never hear about otherwise.

There have been so many times on the group when I've discovered something that had completely passed me by for years on end, and for that I'm very grateful indeed. In fact, I'm very grateful for the group for many reasons, and not least the fact that it has allowed me to geek out about stuff I am seriously into with likeminded individuals round the world. Interaction with these people is always a pleasure. These people GET WHAT IT'S ABOUT, and they UNDERSTAND WHY VHS IS AMAZING. Please excuse the caps there. I needed to raise my voice a bit. Talking about the internet will do that to a person.

The VHS group (or just 'the group' as I refer to it when mentioning it to my long-suffering lady) is a magical place filled with tapes from faraway lands as well as nostalgia and education the likes of which I've rarely found elsewhere online in the million years since I first got onto the internet.

The characters which show up on that page are a wonderfully motley assortment of film fans, stoners, diehard collectors, old-school tapeheads and curious bystanders who pop up for a few comments and then vanish again. It's a lively forum for people with a fetish for an obsolete format, a lifeline for people like me stuck in a place where VHS tapes are getting to be very hard to come by (unless you want thousands of *Friends* videos, *Buffy* tapes or faded old sports videos), keeping me up to date with the weird and wonderful world of VHS collecting.

Actually, I must admit to being hugely jealous of a great number of members of the group. For one thing, most of them have stupendously impressive VHS collections which make my own look like I started a week ago. However, a select few members seem like gods to me, for the simple fact that they got to meet up for the first time in the real world at a cult movie fest over in the USA. Another thing is the availability of the tapes over there in the States.

It still amazes me that collecting VHS horror movies can even be seen as a hobby, as it made me realise that I wasn't alone in doing this weird thing I do, and I am so very grateful for that. So yeah, heres a shout-out to every single member of the Horror VHS Collectors Unite Facebook page for being so argumentative, so passionate and so damn odd. Here's to us, you glorious freaks. How about a movie night sometime?

Speaking of the differences between collectors around the world...

VHS COLLECTORS:
HOW WE DIFFER AROUND THE WORLD

There are some big differences between UK and US collectors, which I shall talk about a little here. I would add the rest of the world to the 'not US collectors' gang too, in that the US scene is so much bigger and so much more fruitful down to the simple fact that the pace is far bigger and had way, WAY more VHS content available over the years, right from the initial boom through to the dark days of Blockbuster and beyond. There was much more content, a massive amount more of the tapes themselves, and an astonishingly high number of outlets both large and small.

Sure, the UK had its fair share of video stores both independent and in chains, but nothing on the scale of the US. To be frank, American collectors have much more hunting ground and way more tapes to be grabbed and enjoyed. This makes for some interesting differences between collectors in different countries. From what I see and hear about US collectors going on VHS hunts, there are still stores in existence which still carry VHS tapes in their stock, or at least have a bundle in storage somewhere, or even stores which sell tons of old ‚voices on various formats.

In the UK, VHS disappeared from commercial shelves almost entirely in maybe 2002 or so. After that, literally the only places which had them available have been charity shops, car boot sales and private sellers on eBay and Amazon. Yet in the US there still seem to be occasional mom and pop stores open, or places which have closed down but are still full of tapes, or places where massive numbers of tapes are being liquidated for next to nothing. And thrift stores, of course. The scavenger spirit, that feeling of rescuing tapes from oblivion, is exactly the same the world over.

We're historians, dammit. Pop culture historians.

The hunger and the fascination is the same the world over, by the expectations seem different to me. Here in the UK we're pretty damn happy finding one or two tapes in the wild and can only dream of massive hauls. I think my biggest ever haul was something like 26 tapes at once. That was like Christmas to me, yet you can regularly see collectors in other countries make massive hits from abandoned video stores, random peoples' basements, old storage units and any number of other places. That proliferation of tape goodness out there in the States makes my film nerd mouth water far more than it should. I'm proud to be English (and NORTHERN, I would like to add), but man, I envy the American VHS fans out there.

It also interests me that there is a definite difference between UK and US collectors' tastes in tapes. In the UK, the main thing that a lot of collectors want to track down is anything from the notorious Video Nasties list that the DPP put together (see the chunk on the subject earlier in this very book). Those things are the grails over here. Those tapes sum up the video era, or at least a sizable portion of it, due to the sheer scale of the controversy at the time. Those tapes are the ones which go for the silly amounts. Of course, other than those it seems the main thing a lot of us want to track down over here are ex-rental tapes in the oversized clamshells we refer to as 'big boxes' (as mentioned, different to the big box tapes in the States), from pretty much any genre you can imagine. Ex-rental tapes are things of beauty as they were the ones we saw on the shelves of the video shops we spent too much time in when growing up. Those things shaped us as film fans and I would certainly argue they helped shape us as people as well to some extent.

In the US, the focus seems to be more on obscure low/no budget fare such as *Tales From The Quadead Zone, 555, Lunchmeat, The Abomination* and similar fare. Or those gorgeous THRILLER VIDEO tapes with Elvira on them. In addition, a lot of US collectors look to other territories for their tape fix, with many collectors having a deep and abiding love for Mexican or Japanese movies and tapes.

THE CHOSEN FEW:
THE PEOPLE KEEPING VHS ALIVE

There are a number of small, independent companies out there who are releasing limited edition VHS tapes of rare movies, as well as those releasing new independent films on the format as well. I cannot commend these people highly enough, as I wouldn't know the first thing about putting a project like that together.

Even back in the day it would have been difficult, but now, with VHS tapes no long being mass produced and technology moving so far away from its analogue roots, it must be even more difficult. Yet still the releases keep coming, directed right at the audience who will love them. Genre fare is the staple of these companies and their releases, which is totally understandable as that's the stuff which will always have a cult following which will want to pick tapes up for their collection.

In addition, the releases look so good that they fit right in with the classic titles that collectors already own. Such is the love for the format shown by the people involved in getting is stuff out. New product looks new, but these tapes have been designed and packaged as they would have been years ago.

While that dedication may be scoffed at by digital media purists, they frankly don't understand. Yes, our numbers are small, but lovers of analogue media love the idea of an item we can hold, something in a case with a cover. That tactile element is one of the things which gives VHS, and indeed its brother in obscurity, vinyl, its longevity with collectors the world over, and these small companies are helping to feed that need for new content.

Examples? Massacre Video is a good starting point. They have released limited run tapes of titles such as the infamous *555, DEMON QUEEN, THE ABOMINATION* and more. The tapes look fantastic, with retro styled covers in their clamshell releases which look perfect alongside genuine vintage tapes. A lot of love has gone into those things. Or how about Horror Boobs Video or the many others?

All of them are doing their bit for the VHS underground with limited video releases, zines and more. Even the VHShitfest blog got in on the act, with videos, zines and more. Of course, the people behind VHShitfest, Horror Boobs and the awesome Lunchmeat VHS magazine were also instrumental in bringing the definitive VHS collector documentary, Adjust Your Tracking, to fruition.

Other names include FRIGHTMARE VIDEO (*NAILGUN MASSACRE...*), CAMP MOTION PICTURES (*THE BASEMENT* box set) and the gloriously named MONDO VIDEO (*SLEDGEHAMMER...*). All of their tapes are beautifully packaged and made with a genuine love for the medium and the era that spawned it.

And then there are dudes like those at Briarwood Entertainment, the guys that made and released new horror fodder like the already-notorious *SLAUGHTER TALES*, made by director Johnny Dickie, who was just 15 at the time the film was made. That flick demonstrates a real love for the video era and its trappings, offering a horror movie which may be cheap and cheesy, but is nevertheless perfect VHS fodder, and has been released in a variety of editions, all of which have been really nicely realised.

Of course, the VHS dream isn't just about tapes, but the appreciation of them as well. Companies like ARROW VIDEO, SHOUT FACTORY, 88 FILMS, NUCLEUS and the like all release high quality DVD and Blu-Ray editions of classic and hard-to-find VHS era movies. A personal favourite is Arrow, who released a series of incredible DVD sets of cult favourites including masses of extra features, posters, art cards, booklets and new art.

Similarly, the VHS era legend grows with documentaries like the excellent *ADJUST YOUR TRACKING* (which I was so stoked to get my name in the credits of – that was a dream come true) and also *REWIND THIS*! Both cover the cultural impact of the VHS tape, rental stores and everything that went with them.

Genre-specific documentaries like the aforementioned *VIDEO NASTIES: THE DEFINITIVE GUIDE* box set, the *SLICE AND DICE* slasher movie documentary or *GOING TO PIECES* (at one point packaged in the UK in a superb triple DVD set of *LAST HOUSE ON THE LEFT*), which look at the horror genre and its explosion throughout the video rental era.

It pleases me greatly that there are younger collectors and enthusiasts getting involved and actually making new content for the format. At present it seems that these companies are all in the US, but that's understandable as the VHS collecting scene is far larger there than anywhere in the world. The important thing to me is that these new releases are done with love and respect for the format and the era which was so very influential on popular culture for so long. Much respect you guys. Thanks for helping us addicts have stuff to fill our shelves with.

THE FUTURE OF VHS HORROR COLLECTING

Is there a future for a hobby which is based entirely around a dead format which is becoming ever harder to find? I do have to wonder, sometimes. Supplies of fresh tapes are becoming harder to find in the wild, and prices are rising online. Now that people have figured out some tapes are actually worth a lot of money to certain collectors, there seems to be an upward surge in people milking collectors for all we're worth.

    The act of bidding things up for the sake of it, or flipping tapes (Flipping is the practice of buying stuff cheap to sell on again at a higher price), or asking ludicrous amounts for tapes does nothing other than harm the hobby and make you seem like an arsehole, in my opinion, anyway. Yes, we as collectors are generally desperate to get our next fix of magnetic tape in a little black box, but we're not stupid. Usually.

    With the format now being evicted from the homes of the world's populace in massive amounts, the time is perfect to snap up some treasures, lest they be dumped into landfill, incinerated or just forgotten. I have always seen it my duty as a collector (and this goes for other things as well as horror VHS tapes) to rescue these items from oblivion, to preserve them and enjoy them and give them the respect they deserve.

    Video tapes ruled the world for a long time when it came to home entertainment, and to allow that massively influential and exciting era to be forgotten or brushed aside seems criminal to me. However, while there have been literally millions of VHS tapes appearing on the market around the world in recent years, that supply will soon dry up.

    Tapes that are sought after will go to collectors and the less desirable tapes will be destroyed or dumped. The remaining popular tapes on online auction sites and suchlike will go up in price due to their increased rarity, and fewer people will be able to collect.

    On one had this would be a good thing, as it means the diehard collectors will be able to still find what they want, but more casual collectors or people with less disposable income (*waves* like me, for example) will be shoved out of a hobby we find hugely enjoyable. That's the worst case scenario, of course. I mean, it could just be that the Hipsters and fakes will be booted out of the hobby and have to move onto some other bit of retro stuff in order to continue to seem kooky and oh-so-ironic.

    So does the hobby have a future? I think so. It will become even more of a niche interest, but it will continue for those of us who remember the era and cherish the items which brought so many people so much pleasure. Sadly, I can't keep up.

    Yeah, VHS has a future, thanks to collectors around the world and the handful of dedicated small companies who release special edition VHS tapes of new and old flicks, and as along as we know those tapes are out there, we'll hunt on. It's ice to know that, while I appear to be the only VHS horror collector locally, there are many likeminded individuals out there who keep the dream alive, and in far grander style than I myself am able.

VHS HORROR COLLECTORS: WE ARE LEGION

Collectors of VHS horror movies aren't limited to one place or one demographic. Men and women of all ages find enjoyment in the bizarre and wonderful world of VHS, from all backgrounds and from a wide range of countries. That's a very cool thought, as it means I'm officially not that weird after all (he types, while wearing a pink clown costume and wings made out of human eyelids stapled together).

However, many collectors out there are far more knowledgeable and experienced with the medium than I am, and I thought it would be a good idea to have the input of some far better collectors than me in here so as to deflect accusations of being a lousy collector away from me, heh.

What follows is a series of candid conversations with a few eminent collectors from around the world, on their love for the format, collecting tapes, the history of their fascination with VHS and more. In talking to people for this section, I found myself humbled and moved by some of the things they told me, as well as some deep envy at their collections. Talking to these people has reminded me that a collection of VHS tapes, in our case horror movies and obscure genre flicks, are much more than just films we watch. They are a kind of autobiographical reminder of the days and years which shaped us as people. They can remind us of good times and bad times along the way, but above all they contain the magic which we all share when enjoying a film. These are my people, and this is what they had to tell me.

IAN EVANS

I feel a great sense of kinship with Ian. He seems like just the sort of collector I am, with similar tastes and a similar sense of humour. Ian's here in the UK and as such shares my own plight in having difficulty finding much of interest in the wild, although he's given me some great tips on places to hunt which had never even occurred to me, like landfill offices and recycling plants. I've known him over a year now, and I still don't know what the guy looks like, even though we've traded and stuff. I keep trying to suggest we set up a UK meet-up of people from the HORROR

VHS COLLECTORS UNITE Facebook page, but as we keep concluding, it'd probably end up being me and him sat in a pub talking about old Medusa and Full Moon tapes.

"I can't compete with the big money collectors, and nor would I want to," he tells me. "It's not about competing anyway, which the hobby seems to be for a lot of people out there. The mentality of 'ooh, VHS is cool now' is really annoying. I've been picking tapes up for years because I love the films and the objects themselves. To me it's not a case of 'Look at how awesome my collection is', more a case of 'look at all the stuff I found that I love the shit out of.'"

This is an opinion I do share, to be honest. I love the idea of making a bundle on tapes, but 98% of my video hunting is for my own pleasure rather than financial gain. I'm not immune to the lure of cash (who is?), but it's never been my main focus.

"I think my favourite tapes are the *Children of the Corn* one I got for 20p, my old M.R. James tapes of TV stuff and that pre-cert *Mad Max* you sold me."

Yeah, I collect the stuff I *want*, not stuff that will get me some kind of status.

"That's what it's all about, man!"

None of my stuff was very expensive. Some of my favourites: Lemme think, *The Video Dead* was about 6 quid, *Neon Maniacs* about a tenner, *Arcade* was 2.99 and my *Generation X* was 7.99 bought from the video shop two days after it came out as they liked me and did me a deal. VHS to me is nostalgic and fun. It's not a money game. I'm into this stuff because I spent most of my teenage years wandering around video shops.

"Same here! That's what I thought it was about too. I collected on my own for years. I didn't know anybody else into it, it was just like my thing that I did. It's not, y'know... I don't want to be part of any scene. I just love finding tapes and sharing them with guys like you."

I love the historical and nostalgic aspect of it too. These things were so important to our lives.

"Yeah, I remember renting *E.T.* With my dad and seeing Pinhead staring down at me from a *Hellraiser* tape. I remember that really clearly. That and being too young to rent the stuff I really wanted to see. The DPP list tapes had long gone by then as well, so it's all post-cert stuff I remember from my early days. The interest in pre-certs and the Video Nasties came later. I actually went and stole the empty case for *Bad Taste* from a video shop in my old town and had my mates brother rent it and rig up a Scart to Scart copy on VHS just so I could own my own copy! I feel pretty bad about that, really. However, they always used to give you the films in those shitty photocopied yellow sleeves covered in adverts for window cleaners and farm auctions. At least around here anyway. A big rubber-faced alien flipping the finger was much cooler to me. So, when I was 18, I didn't buy cider, I went and signed up for a rental account and pretty much cleared out all the horror section for the next few months. Then when Woolworth's started selling the sell through tapes I just started buying them and I guess the collection went from there. It's always been about collecting stuff I loved, or stuff I would have loved then if I'd had the chance, you know?"

Indeed I do, mate. Indeed I do.

ROB LANE
(STRAIGHT TO VIDEO)

Rob Lane is the mastermind behind the STRAIGHT TO VIDEO project, a music project which pays tribute to the awesome songs that can be found on movie soundtracks. The bassist (who has played with TEENAGE CASKET COMPANY, BULLETBOYS, LET LOOSE and more) brought together a bunch of likeminded musicians from a variety of acts (Including Enuff Z'nuff, Bowling For Soup and more) and put out a frankly brilliant EP including covers of tracks from sources as eclectic as *Pretty In Pink, Clerks 2* and *A Nightmare On Elm Street 4: The Dream Master*! Regarding the EP, Rob says in the press release: "I wanted an unashamedly fun project that represented every element of the things I love, particularly what I grew up with and made me - ME! I wanted a huge melting pot of music, film, nostalgia and fun - with no apologies!"

He's a massive movie fan, and is instrumental in the running of the regular 80s movie night by the same name of STRAIGHT TO VIDEO, which is where I met him during a screening of the brilliant US documentary *ADJUST YOUR TRACKING*.

"I will always look back on VHS as an adventure. You really never knew what you were gonna get," Rob tells me with a huge grin. "Long before the days of the internet where you can now find reviews or scour YouTube for Trailers and spoilers, your local video shop would have racks upon racks of films you'd never heard of before. Weird and wonderful artwork would entice you to grab one of these masterpieces from the shelf before taking it to the counter in the hope that you could hire an 18 Certificate film at only ten years old! Of course you always could, no problem. Everyone knew which video shops would hire out to kids, it was no big deal."

Nostalgia certainly plays its part in the recent VHS boom we've seen of late.

"Like most things in the 1980s, video has that magical feeling when you look back upon it. Anything was up for grabs, it was a fun time before things became overly packaged, processed and slick. You'd always come home with something to watch, whether it be the current blockbuster film which you'd had on reserve for two or three weeks because the shop only had the one copy, or perhaps you had to take that gamble on the some dusty slasher flick that was a third generation *Friday the 13th*, who cared? You were watching a video that night! That was awesome and I miss that."

You can find out more about the Straight To Video project – and the awesome EP available in a VHS case – at www.straighttovideo.co.uk

JOSH SCHAFER
(LUNCHMEAT VHS MAGAZINE)

Josh Schafer is the editor in chief for the frankly brilliant LUNCHMEAT VHS print magazine and site (visit the main site at **www.lunchmeatvhs.com**) over in the US, and is known as both a devout VHS collector and a very cool guy. Enthusiastic almost to the point of a very pleasant mania, the guy certainly knows his tapes. So Josh mate, what keeps you interested in the VHS format?

"VHS is something that's always been in my life. It was the format that I watched as a kid, and as I grew older, I just never stopped watching it. VHS has enabled me to find so many flicks, especially the weirdo / cult / super-obscure stuff lingering in the deepest abysses of cinema. So many amazing (and not-so-amazing!) flicks are only available on the VHS format, and for every diehard film fan, VHS is truly indispensable. Beyond the nostalgia and the video-only merits, I just really love the aesthetics of VHS. From the vibrant and fun artwork to the weathered and dingy feel of the analog tape... it's just an experience I've always favoured over anything else. I stay interested because all of these charms still hold true for me. I'm still finding new flicks all the time, still loving the amazing artwork, and now, with the re-birth of this rabid collecting culture and new wave VHS releases, it's allowed me to make even more cool stuff and meet truly fantastic people who I'm proud to call my friends. It's truly something beautiful, and I would never want to lose it."

What drives you on with the Lunchmeat fun?

"It's just what you said: FUN! I mean, when LM first started, it was all about the flicks. As I mentioned, there are SO MANY flicks, especially of the cult / fringe persuasion, that are only available on video, and will most likely NEVER make it to any other format. LM celebrates those kinds of films, reviews them, and wants to share them out with the folks that care about that sort of thing. And now, with all of the culture rising up, I've had the opportunity to be involved with so many groovy projects e.g. releasing new wave home video releases, acting in films, co-producing a documentary on VHS collecting, screenings galore… it's just a blast. And, I mean, who would have thought!? If you were to tell me 5 years ago that all of this would be happening, I would be ecstatic… but I would think you were high off your ass, too (laughs). It's been an amazing experience thus far, and I don't plan on stopping. Honestly, being creative is what makes me happy, makes me thrive, and the fact that I have this pulpit to speak from, a brand to help spread the love of VHS, it's a gift.

And though I've worked really hard, I don't take it for granted. It might sound corny, but VHS brings me a lot of happiness, and anything I can do to help it live on and give it the chance to bring someone else happiness, then I'm all about it. Plus, I just like making stuff (laughs). And the people I've met through all this… we're like a family now. We're all in this together… whatever it is!"

And what would be a few of your favourite tapes? I know that's opening quite a can of worms!

"Well, *MICROWAVE MASSACRE* on Midnight Video and *MOTHER'S DAY* on some fly-by-night budget label are among my personal favourites in my collection, just because they were some of the first tapes that I bought that really made me fall in love with collecting. For their personally historical importance (laughs) they always have a special place for me. But, I mean, I think my favorites are really always changing. I think that's part of the fun of collecting. I see mad groovy stuff online and I want, no, NEED IT! Then, I'll be out on the hunt in the wild, and come across something I never knew existed and just be head over heels about this random budget tape from 1987. So many favorites, and it's always expanding and contracting. It's a veritable love affair, indeed. But as far as a concrete answer I would say all of the Chop 'Em Ups videos, especially *INQUISITION*. That's out of my price range now, though. I'm really into the Star Classics illustrated covers like *PLANET OF BLOOD, POOR PRETTY EDDIE* and *BLOOD LEGACY.* I just love the cheapo yet mesmerizing nature of those covers! But as far as a supreme Holy Grail as it were, I really still don't know. Like I said, it's always changing… I just know I'll see something tomorrow on the Horror VHS Collectors Unite! page and be like, "DAMN! THAT SHIT IS SO DOPE!" and then I'll drool for a while, then find something else that drives me wild. And, that, right there, is why I love VHS: It's non-stop excitement, love and happiness."

DEATH WOUND ZINE

I got in touch with the mysterious W from Death Wound zine for the simple fact that the zine is one of the best I've ever seen. With an old-school mix of cut and paste aesthetics and a raucous mix of horror, VHS, weird articles and a love of black metal and other extreme music, the magazine is unique and looks incredible, coming with a toe-tag attached to it and more. I asked about the importance and influence of VHS and horror movies, and this is what W had to say.

"Cult and genre films, but particularly horror, have a long tradition that is built upon legacy and an adoration of the past. In contrast, the major blockbusters of the past twenty years or so do not cherish the past, and impose a rather longsighted vision of the future that often falls short. While this may seem vague I suppose, think of god damn *Avatar*, about those blue space aliens. I mean, look at it objectively. It was a major success in terms of the box office, but I hope to never again think about the intellectual seppuku I committed watching that flick, ya know? There's no context and tradition...I mean I guess there is, if a bloated CGI budget is the tradition. And that's the problem with the bulk of major studio films made today. It's a cultural product, that has no acknowledgement of where it comes from.

Genre films are different. There's such a trajectory you can trace and see by watching all these movies. Cannibal flicks...mondo films...there's a history that is so easy to uncover, and you can just get lost in it, and all these films draw from each other. Ultimately, that's why I love VHS. The box size, adjusting the tracking, the grain...and dare I say, the jamming of a tape that results in popped blood vessels and a broken VCR? That's how the majority of genre film viewers watched movies for so many years. And that's important to remember, in the sense that we wouldn't have access to all of these amazing films, if it weren't for the home video market. So for me, it's not just about collecting, but an entire experience I have, and a little nod to the experience I had as a youth, and enjoy to look back on.

And what about Death Wound? Where did that stem from?

"As far as the zine, I wrote it because I realized that I was watching all these movies with nothing tangible to show for it. Not in the sense that I wanted to express my opinion about films...every jackass on the internet does that every few minutes. Going with the experiential reasons for my love of VHS, I wanted to present an aesthetic and textual experience in a format I value the most, which is printed material. It seems sort of bizarre to write about an "outdated" format and movies that are forty years old, but type it all up on the internet and have people comment. Writing is sort of tyrannical. Somebody can put it down in print, but they usually don't throw it out. And that's important...your writing and visual presentation remains. So were VHS rentals, in a sort of diluted sense. You rent some Wizard VHS at your local video store, and think it will be the coolest thing ever. And you put it on and it sucks but that's the total charm of it. That although so many movies are horrible, you've already rented it, and nothing can be done. A blog, a digital rental or a download are so easily discarded."

W pauses, reflective.

"You know, there's that scene in *Maniac* where Frank Zito talks about how he likes the photographer's portraits, because she's preserving them forever and they become her property. I don't think that's true about photographs, but I think there's some twisted way we try to build OUR OWN legacies in text and/or visual mediums. A zine has a visual presentation you can't get on the internet, and even if somebody just likes the pictures and layout, good for them. That's how the greatest films I ever rented on VHS got me hooked in the first place, and to share that with even one person, is worthy of doing."

- W.

Death Wound Zine

PETER ROBERTSON

Peter is one of the nicest guys you could hope to speak to, and I hope he's doing well. This interview was conducted before the mayhem kicked off in Turkey in 2013, where he currently lives and works, and I haven't heard from him in too long. As well as being a fine gent, Peter is one of the most knowledgable and enthusiast collectors I know, and has provided me with some films I never thought I'd ever have copies of. His own VHS collection is spectacular, but even more spectacular are his reminiscences of the VHS era and the Video Nasties era. I could have talked to him all night. It only took moments before we were talking tapes.

"I got some new cassettes today, I was just checking them out when you came onto Skype."

He reels off the list of new tapes and I become even more jealous of him than I already am.

"I got into it in the mid-eighties. I was always interested in horror films, always reading stuff like Fangoria, and back in the eighties I remember Dad actually renting a video player from a shop and a few tapes. The first videos we had were copies of *The Exterminator* and *The Alchemist*, so basically a Robert Ginty double bill. I was terrified by The Alchemist at the time, but there was that feeling I was seeing something I shouldn't. Doing something a little bit naughty. I remember going to school around the age of 15 and used to pop to see a friend of mine, Leslie, whose mum could get copies of all of the Video Nasties, and he would show me the best bits of those films, *I Spit On Your Grave* and suchlike, fast-forwarding through all the dialogue. Each one ended up lasting about twenty minutes! I had no idea what they were, what they were called, but I remember coming away from his house traumatized (laughs)."

Kind of like the compilation that was shown to members of parliament during the Video Nasties scandal – just all of the violence, completely out of context.

"I actually wanted to see more, but we had to watch them in these like twenty minute slots before his mum got back from work. So then I remember going to WHSmith and seeing the release of *An American Werewolf In London*. I remember really wanting it, to see it and just hold the thing. We joined a local video shop and that's where the real interest in genre films started. All my money went on renting films. One day I convinced them to sell me a copy of something I loved, and soon after I discovered a stall on a local market which had films, and I was on my way. It wasn't until I met another collector, a guy called Simon, that I learned more about the banned films. This was before the internet of course. You had to know someone who knew these things! I got a bunch of my early titles from him and developed a list of stuff I wanted, which I would search for on the market stalls. I'd come back with some real gems from there, and also bought some from Simon too."

It's a weird feeling finding other collectors.

"I remember a fanzine called In The Flesh, by this guy called Steve, done on a typewriter, which was brilliant. It contained a section where you could write in and introduce yourself and tell people you were looking for certain films. A few more came that way. I started driving around in my old van, going round all of the video shops I could find, looking for films I needed. I'd go down to the Electric Ballroom sometimes, and met a guy really big, threatening guy there called Bill who arranged to meet up to let me look through some films. This guy was a little scary, and so when I went along I had a friend come with me. I mean, I was 19 at the time and had no idea what to expect. The guy opened his door and instantly there was a big Bulldog snapping at us. He ushered us in and gave us a tour of his place, which was... interesting. In order to get to the video room we had to go through the weapons room."

Weapons? Crikey.

"Yeah, crossbows, knives, revolvers. He used to sell them to people. He offered us some knives, but we very politely told him we were just looking for films (laughs). We ended up in this back room stacked high with every film you could imagine at the time, and bought a couple and traded a couple. I just wanted to get out alive!"

Now that sounds iffy. I know a lot of other collectors out there have similar stories.

"Yeah! And then I used to have a market stall myself in Milton Keynes, selling movie posters and postcards and stuff. There was a couple of guys there at the market selling copies of horror movies. I was pretty careful myself, not selling copies of things in public. I didn't want to get caught or anything. Anyway, I realized one day that a bunch of people were hanging around the edges of the market, keeping an eye on the stall these guys had. The next week they were busted for selling pirate copies of stuff like *Cannibal Ferox* and porn movies. I mean, I had my own customers for stuff but never sold them in public. Just private. In fact that helped pay for my teaching course. Customers ended up as friends, staying in touch for years."

Much like collectors do now, right around the world.

"Exactly. However, it seems that one day someone had tipped the police off that I was doing something with dodgy films. This was just before I moved to Istanbul to teach. I was going to pack up all my films and put them in storage and come away for a year. This guy came up at the stall and started asking about the films, but I wouldn't give him any info. Then the same night the same guy showed up at my place and asked again in a really odd manner. I said look, I have a few pirate tapes but only in my own collection. I wouldn't try to sell them, y'know? But what I had downstairs was a copy of *Texas Chainsaw 2* which I tried to get rid of him with. I didn't hear from him for a few days, then he brought it back randomly. My neighbour recognized him as one of the officers from the police station she worked at! Soon she warned me that it looked like the authorities were checking me out. I immediately shipped all my films elsewhere, moved out of my house and moved to Istanbul. Literally two days later I heard that the police had arrived to look at my stuff and found and empty house! In the end, my old friend Simon got picked up for pirate tapes but was let off, but he had a friend who actually went to prison due to tapes and a previous record. I decided I didn't want to lose my collection, but it seemed silly that they were just sitting there in storage, so every time I came back to England I took home ten films or so at a time. I wasn't collecting though. The collecting kicked back in when I discovered eBay!"

Oh man, I can relate to that. If ever a site was made for sad old collectors like us...

"All I was doing was getting my old stuff out of storage, but I didn't want to give up on it. It's one of those things where you can have good days and bad days in your life, but the tapes are always there. The films are always there. And everything else about them helps. There's something about the covers, the artwork, the trailers. I don't mean you'll regularly sit down and watch *SS Experiment Camp* in the name of having a good time (laughs)."

Things like that are more like artifacts.

"Yeah. It's part of this underground. There's a mystique about these films. Even though they came out on DVD or whatever, the format is still... I don't know. Holding a tape, you actually fell like you're holding a film in your hand. There's a connection there. These things gave me an identity back at high school, back when there were geek groups and punk groups and whatever else. I was kind of a loner but had my film 'thing' going on. Part of it may have been wanting to be cool, as I used to stage film nights showing Evil Dead and stuff, that got me a bit of street cred, but I didn't think I was doing anything bad with tapes. I didn't really think it was illegal at the time. It seemed wrong, but something that much fun surely couldn't be wrong, could it?"

Hell no. I couldn't have said it better myself.

25 Cult Movies You Should See On VHS

Presented here is a run-down of 25 cult movies you really should see on VHS if at all possible. This is by no means a comprehensive list, as for one thing that would take up an entire book in itself (hmm... There's an idea...) and for another, any such list is somewhat subjective. These are thus 25 of the films I feel sum up my own experience of the VHS era well, and most can be enjoyed on DVD/Blu-Ray/Streaming/Whatever's big by the time you read this.

However, for the full effect, I believe they are at their most effective when viewed in a 4:3 ratio, on an old TV and a VCR which has temperamental tracking. Many are cheesy beyond belief, with lapses in internal logic and bad production values galore, but that's the beauty of the medium and the cinematic era which spawned it. It was FUN, and remains so to this day.

Grab some cold ones, some form of salted snack, and kick back with some vintage violence which far outclasses the era which followed it. Keep your mind open, and be reminded that there was a whole universe of entertainment out there before CGI, shaky-cam and bullet-time spoiled everything.

These are the VHS tapes which ate my brain.

A Nightmare on Elm Street 3: Dream Warriors (1987)
The second sequel to the original NOES is a near-perfect horror movie in which a group of troubled teens in an institute band together to wage war against Freddy – with epic results. Heather Langenkamp returns from the original, alongside John Saxon, and newcomer Patricia Arquette is fantastic as the new lead, Kristen. The theme tune by 80s melodic hard rock legends DOKKEN is a masterpiece in itself, perfectly rounding out a flat-out brilliant horror movie. The effects and style may have dated, but its power remains.

Basket Case (1982)

Frank Henenlotter's grindhouse classic is essential viewing. It's dirty and cheap and stuffed with atmosphere, and boasts a wicked sense of humour. What's in the basket? Belial's in there, and he's one pissed-off blob. Surprisingly creepy, thanks to some decent casting and inventive use of the limited budget. Where else can you see someone offed with a face full of scalpels?

Killer Klowns From Outer Space (1988)

The title says it all, really. An amazing piece of comedy-horror entertainment in which a bunch of demented alien clowns wreak havoc on an unsuspecting town. Brilliant in every possible way, from the costumes and awful puns to the gloriously demented interior of the Klowns' spaceship.

The Video Dead (1987)

An awesome low-budget flick in which zombies trapped in an old film are able to cross over into our world via an old TV set. Mayhem ensues, despite a weak middle act. One of the true classics of the VHS horror era, and definitely one of the coolest pieces of cover art you will ever see (a zombie erupting from a TV set). At points it plays like a comedy but it remains an excellent watch.

Neon Maniacs (1986)

This was one of my favourite rentals. A dozen demonic, rubber-faced monsters show up seemingly for no reason and start butchering people. Nonsensical, but lots of fun, and it has amazing cover art. In fact, the cover art alone is reason enough to track this gem down for your collection. The Uk big-box tape looks amazing.

Trick or Treat (1986)

One of my favourite films of all time, as it mixes two of my passions – 1980s horror and old-school heavy metal. The resulting film is a massive amount of cheesy fun, and watch out for cameos from Ozzy Osbourne and Gene Simmons. I actually went and bought a bunch of the albums you see onscreen in Eddie's room, and discovered some brilliant music through that film. I have a *Trick Or Treat* shrine developing in the house actually, with the original UK rental tape, the soundtrack on CD, the soundtrack on vinyl framed up, a T-shirt and an early one-sheet poster also framed up. I missed out on winning a press pack from it on eBay recently, and could have screamed.

Zombie Flesh Eaters
Lucio Fulci's glorious masterpiece of voodoo and zombie mayhem, known just as *ZOMBIE* in America. Sort of an unofficial sequel to *Dawn Of The Dead*, but with none of the cast, no plot links, and loads more gore. It has some truly terrible acting and lines in it, but the scenes of zombie carnage are a nasty glory to behold, and it is shot with such style that Lucio Fulci's detractors really do have no argument here.

Street Trash (1987)
Ahh, *Street Trash*. A bunch of drunks and gloriously un-PC caricatures of homeless tramps start drinking a strange old liquor called Viper, and then they start exploding, melting and turning into blobs of goo. And there are two minutes of this film which consist of tramps playing catch around a junkyard with a severed penis. How can you not watch it?

The Gate (1985)
Two kids open a gateway to a hellish dimension by playing subliminal messages on cult metal records. I had no choice but to love this film. It's brilliant. The sequel wasn't that great, but this first one was a near masterpiece of 1980s horror and pop culture, with the added bonus of some impressive effects sequences and creepy stop-motion animation. Almost perfect.

Necropolis: City of the Dead (1987)
This ultra cheap supernatural horror movie sees a witch resurrected after 300 years laying waste to hookers, vagrants and

more in order to feed her zombie pets ectoplasm from her six boobs. I am not kidding. That's an actual scene. If a Madonna/ Lady GaGa lookalike killing people and lactating KY Jelly is your thing, then check it out. Also notable for a very clearly failed squib during a shooting, where the actor notices the failed effect and THEN reacts to being 'shot', with the failed squib sticking out of his shirt. Still, I loved this trashy gem.

Vamp (1986)
Featuring Grace Jones as a superbly creepy vampire stripper, this film is a massive amount of fun set in a strip club full of bloodsuckers. It has a gloriously tacky 80s colour palette (lots of pink or green lighting) and that unique mix of comedy and horror that the era did so well.

NEMESIS (1992)
Albert Pyun's cyberpunk classic is a delight from start to finish. Possibly the most perfect straight to video science fiction action movie ever made. Olivier Gruner, Brion James, cyborgs, long coats and a hell of a lot of fighting. A low budget masterpiece. Just don't expect the same thing from its three sequels! The first sequel, *NEMESIS 2: NEBULA* is watchable, but *NEMESIS 3: TIME LAPSE* is a mess and *NEMESIS 4: CRY OF ANGELS* is just plain weird. The first one remains a fantastic piece of 90s grindhouse style sci-fi.

ARCADE (1993)
Starring Megan Ward, Seth Green and John DeLancie, this fun tale of a Virtual Reality video game gone haywire remains a pleasure to watch. It has the atmosphere of a Point Horror novel by R.L. Stine, mixed with bits of *Tron*. A gem, despite its miniature budget and the painfully dated CG effects. Here and now it almost looks like a Nickelodeon TV movie, but I still hold it dear to my heart. I fell in love with the pre-release poster for it on the back of an imported horror mag when I was 14 and discovered a rental tape of it for sale cheap while on holiday in '93. It met my expectations at the time, and it still keeps me

grinning now.

BRAIN DAMAGE (1988)
A wise-cracking parasitic turd-like creature feeds the lead character a mad hallucinogenic drug to make him its slave and bring him fresh victims to suck the brains out of. What's not to love? Directed by *Basket Case* helmsman Frank Henenlotter, this is a horror comedy with lots of horror and plenty of comedy, that rare breed of film which gets the blend of the two exactly right. Trippy, gory and funny, it's a must-see.

SPOOKIES (1985)
Turd monsters that fart while chasing people. What else do you need to know? This fun and kitsch piece of 1980s teen horror tomfoolery is actually scenes from a failed horror movie which a distributor bought and added new scenes to, making for a weird 'two films going on at once' feeling. The variations on the cover art to this are amazing. The film ain't brilliant, but it's perfect VHS night fodder.

FRIDAY THE 13TH PART VI: JASON LIVES (1986)
Jason is back from his grave, and some hapless teens are heading into theirs! A soundtrack featuring Alice Cooper, Jason being brutal and a fantastic showdown with the now-grown-up Tommy Jarvis add up to a most pleasant slice of 80s slasher trash. Despite being rather generic at times, its entertainment value makes up for what the script lacks.

CREEPOZOIDS (1987)
A post-apocalyptic *Alien* knockoff, this film is nonetheless a nice slice of dumb fun, mixing a nice simple sci-fi plot (a group of army deserters take shelter from acid rain in an abandoned scientific facility and fall foul of the horrors lurking within) with some nicely gloopy monster and gore effects. It was also where, back when I first saw it in the 1990s, I was first exposed to scream queen Linnea Quigley, who doesn't put in the best performance in the film (that honour goes to the animatronic

Creepozoid baby), but she was in it enough for the teenage me to take a shine to her. The poor woman. The film actually holds up better than you might expect, considering its meagre budget and obvious limitations. It's relatively short (around 75 minutes) and as such gets in there, does what it's supposed to and gets the credits rolling. It's a bad movie, but a bad movie that I still love.

RETURN OF THE LIVING DEAD (1985)

While *Creepozoids* might have been my first exposure to Linnea Quigley, a lot of people around the world saw her first in this glorious horror/comedy hybrid, in which she plays the punk Trash, part of a gang of misfit kids who get caught up in a zombie attack following a military chemical – Trioxin – being released into the atmosphere. Anarchic, witty, funny, gory, fast-paced and featuring that infamous dance sequence atop a tomb, it's easy to forget it's an unofficial pseudo-sequel to George Romero's original *Night of The Living Dead*, even though it's John Russo behind it rather than George himself. *Return of the Living Dead* is a note-perfect example of 80s horror to enjoy on VHS, from the artwork and visuals to the soundtrack and the tongue-in-cheek performances. Just disengage your braaaaaiiiinnnsss.

NIGHT OF THE DEMONS (1988)

Of the three original *Night of the Demons* movies and the 2009 remake, nothing tops the original 1988 film, and that's not just due to my teenaged thing for Linnea Quigley. Yup, it's another Linnea movie, but it's on the list mainly because it's such a blast to watch. A bunch of typical 80s horror movie teens head to a Halloween party in a delightfully tacky spooky old house, and get more than they bargained for when their host, Angela, turns out to be rather more than she seems. Using a ton of 80s camera tricks to spice up the cinematography, along with some spectacular gore and prosthetic effects, *Night of the Demons* is up there with *Return Of The Living Dead* as being a brilliant example of how much fun you can have with VHS genre movie. I love this flick dearly.

DEMONS (1985)

Directed by Lamberto Bava and produced by some guy called Dario Argento (I believe he makes movies or something), this film has one of my favourite concepts ever. A crowd is lured to an old cinema for a free screening of a secret new movie. While watching the horror flick onscreen, the demons of the film escape from the screen and mayhem ensues with the crowd trapped in the building suddenly having to fight for their lives. *Demons* is a ridiculous amount of fun. It's messy, gory, fast-paced and utterly ludicrous. It's so mad and so fun that you can easily forgive the patchy cast and at times sloppy direction. By no means high art, *Demons* is nevertheless a bona fide classic of the video era, full of green-slime-spewing demons with rows of jagged fangs. The sequel is fun too, but not to the same extent. And ignore anything labelled as *Demons 3*, as no third film was officially released. Those are other flicks with the title tagged on for the hell of it. However, the Argento-produced movie *The Church* was intended to be the third official *Demons* movie. Weird how things turn out, eh?

C.H.U.D. (1984)

Much derided by some and much loved by others, this mutants-in-the-sewers movie is a fine example of prime-time VHS genre fodder. While its lousy sequel may have sullied is name even further than its own production values already had, the flick remains thoroughly entertaining. Some great monster effects and some less-than-great performances add up to a standard in most VHS collectors' stashes. I rented it back in the day due to the frankly superb cover art, and was very pleased indeed with the contents of the film itself.

Ninja The Protector (1986)

My favourite of Jospeh Lai's cut-and-paste ninja movies, Ninja The Protector is a typical example of those films. A gang warfare movie from Hong Kong cut together with scenes of white guys as luridly costumed superhero style ninjas kick the crap out of each other. Violence, sex, hilarious dubbing and absolutely no plot whatsoever. Bliss.

TRANCERS (1985)
Directed by Empire Pictures head honcho (later to open Full Moon Pictures/Features) Charles Band, *Trancers* is a rare thing in the pantheon of low-budget cult genre stuff in that it's a surprisingly good film. Of course, it's also a ton of fun and mixes sci-fi with old-fashioned noir, but with Tim Thomerson and Helen Hunt in the leads, a goofy but entertaining time travel story about a future cop going back in time to take on a futuristic zombie cult and some nicely handled photography, it's a cut above. Sure, it looks like a TV movie now and the five sequels (well, five and a bit if you include the 'proper' sequel, which was a 25 minute story filmed for inclusion in an unfinished anthology called *Pulse Pounders*. That segment has now been released as a standalone online).

RE-ANIMATOR (1985)
Another Empire Pictures release, Stuart Gordon's adaptation of the H.P. Lovecraft story is a delight from start to finish. Jeffrey Combs stars as the titular mad scientist who has developed a serum which can reanimate dead bodies. The mixture of horror and comedy is perfect, as are the many outrageous gore effects which live on long after the last frame has faded to black. I mean, how can you not love a film in which the innards of a headless corpse try to strangle someone? If you like horror movies, then i's pretty much impossible not to love *Re-Animator*.

THE DEADLY SPAWN (1983)
One of the most beloved of VHS tapes for serious and semi-serious collectors has got to be this z-grade chunk of messy video evil. Otherwise known as *Return of the Aliens: The Deadly Spawn* or a variation of that, this film is basically a cheap horror movie with a sci-fi element which was marketed as a cash-in on Ridley Scott's timeless *Alien*. That bit of trivia aside, The Deadly Spawn is a lovely bit of trash cinema in which alien monsters (which resemble dicks with teeth) tear people apart after crash

landing on Earth and needing to multiply and spread its race across the planet. Of course, the action is small scale, the production values are completely bargain basement and the gore is unconvincing, but that's where the charm of the film lies. It still manages to be thoroughly entertaining while being thoroughly awful at the same time. And that, dear friends, sums up VHS cult entertainment to me. We know this stuff is often less than brilliant, but there's still so much fun to be had with it.

END CREDITS:
HOW VHS ATE MY BRAIN

The movie ends. The demons are vanquished. The evil robot explodes. The killer is unmasked and hacked to pieces. The heroes high five and the frame freezes as their hands meet. The first notes of the credits song kick in, and the names begin to roll.

So here we are. This is the future. We're older, perhaps a smidgen wiser, and on a personal note slightly bitter and jaded, but still the tapes are rolling and the static clearing to make way for onscreen treats. I scrapped the original ending to this book as it just didn't ring true. In that ending, I was giving up on the hobby. This would be my ending to being a tape collector. I would always love the VHS format and the films that it brought me, but the time had come to stop buying the tapes and to thin down the collection to the essentials. I still may pare the collection down somewhat, but I've decided I'm not going to stop. I don't think I can do that.

VHS tapes are as much a part of who I am and what I do as playing guitar, eating bacon or wearing black t-shirts. Some things are just constant throughout life, and the presence of VHS in my days as a pop culture addict feels autobiographical. The tapes I still have from being a kid work perfectly. The image and sound may be lo-fi, but there are chunks of my life encased in those little black plastic boxes with their white spools and their copyright warning stickers.

Even tapes which contain the most depraved and

demented horror movies hold a sentimental value. Sure, some tapes are valuable and some aren't even worth small change, but the value really isn't important. It's the practice of preserving these things which have been such an influence and provided so much solace over the years. I feel duty bound to rescue tapes as they were always there for me when I needed them and now it's my turn to return the favour. Yeah, anthropomorphizing video tapes as little mind-saving entities which kept me sane during the bad times probably makes me sound even more odd than I really am, but so be it. VHS tapes are amazing things. Am I wasting my time collecting dusty old videos? No. It's something I have enjoyed for a very long time, and I don't see my interest in it fading any time soon. That said, now that I am a father, I have far less free time and available money to dedicate to seeking old tapes in the wild and online, but that's okay, as it means I have to be more discerning with my purchases and not just buy any old crap for the sake of it.

  Sure, if the opportunity presents itself then I'll pick up a big batch, but only if it's full of stuff I want or I know I can circulate to other collectors. However, I do feel that the hobby is going to become more difficult to maintain as the next few years wear on. VHS tapes are becoming ever more scarce, well, they are if you're looking for anything other than *Friends* sitcom tapes, *Star Trek* tapes, copies of *Jerry Maguire* or endless failed romantic comedies. I do sometimes wonder if I should draw a line under the hobby and move on, maybe slim down my collection to the absolute bare essentials for reasons of space and sanity.

  Maybe it's time to do that after all, to call it a day. I have most of the tapes I've always wanted, and a bunch which I'm not too attached to but which look nice on the shelves, so I'm in two minds whether to keep at it or not, really. One thing's for sure though if my collection does shrink and I move on from looking or tapes everywhere, I will never forget the influence VHS has had on my life and the lives of other obscure film lovers around the world. Meeting and talking to a lot of other collectors has reminded me just how deep this stuff ran, how much of an impact it had on the world and popular culture, and just how sad it is that this wonderful format, which is proving to be far more durable and lasting than many originally thought, is being forgotten.

Somehow I cannot see DVDs and suchlike having the same longevity in the hearts of enthusiasts around the world – they feel too throwaway. I do love the newer formats, but without wanting to sound like one of those vinyl snobs talking about old Bob Dylan and Pink Floyd records, I do believe that newer formats lack the personality and presence of a VHS tape. So far, nothing has been able to replicate the thrill of popping open a video case and hearing those chunky sounds of a tape going into the machine, followed by the moments where the tracking rights itself and another adventure begins, preceded by a copyright warning, naturally.

VHS collecting is about far more than picking up bad old films cheaply. It's about reminding us all about an era which is gone, a time of our lives and a time in the evolution of popular culture which was so very vibrant that it continues to hold our attention.

I have had a video recorder in my bedroom from the age of ten years old, and ever since then built up a collection which evolved and changed and became an accurate barometer of where I was at any given moment in my life. In fact, that same VCR now sits in our master bedroom in the house I own with my wife, and is still used daily for my regular nightly fix of VHS goodness from the shelves and cases and stacks beside it.

There are times when I want to get rid of all of them, sever all of my ties to the past, throw the lot away, but the ghosts refuse to be exorcised. Horror has always been a mainstay of that collection, but there were years when a ton of sci-fi was there, or a ton of TV comedy, or a ton of martial arts movies, but there was always VHS. It's always been there when I needed to escape, be it from the hooligans that plagued my neighbourhood when I was a kid, the turbulence of my teenage years, my ruined and unpleasant twenties and now into my rather more sane and stable thirties. Like vinyl fans with their love of cover art and their attention to catalogue numbers, editions, pressings and suchlike,

VHS collectors are at once extremely nerdy and fountains of arcane pop culture knowledge. It's down to us to keep the legacy of VHS alive and keep it known just what a massive influence it had on our lives and continues to do in echoes even now.

VHS collector culture has grown over the past few years, but not just because it's become a fad or something kitsch for fans of retro media to be all fashionable about. It's grown for the simple reason that the people who love tapes and cult movies are finally discovering that they're not alone. There are others out there, just like us, looking through second hand tapes in charity shops and at flea markets and on eBay and Amazon and in trading groups and pages like Horror VHS Collectors Unite! We're all over the world, in cities big and small, with our shelves full of clamshells, slips, big boxes and ex rentals, our walls covered with vintage posters and video ads, and our heads full of 90 minute dreams which begin with a copyright warning, some trailers, a fizzle of screen noise and then the opening credits to the heights of our imagination as well as the depths of our darkest fantasies. VHS brought the strange and wonderful to the masses, and those tapes are waiting out there for us, to be found, rescued, played, kept safe and admired. Then maybe traded. Or sold if you're so inclined.

The availability of VHS in the wild, at least in England, is shrinking very fast indeed. All of the usual places I would be able to find gold-mines of VHS treasure are drying up before my very eyes. Sure, I'm thrilled that other collectors are out there picking up tapes and giving them good, loving homes, but the whole era of 'Retro' stuff being fashionable is driving me nuts. I hate seeing stuff being picked up as a passing fad, when it meant so much to a generation. A lot of people picking tapes up for the sake of it didn't live the era, didn't spend endless hours in video shops trying to figure out what to rent or buy. While there are a lot of younger collectors doing it for the love of the films and the format, there are also a lot of bandwagon jumpers who want to get in on the next cheesy fashion statement. Plus, I have set out to do what I always wanted to do with VHS collecting, and gather copies of the tapes I remember from that magical upstairs room at Metro Video back in my hometown. Some of my tapes are the original ones I rented, and that pleases me so much. I rescued them, just like VHS collectors around the world are doing all the time. I will still love, read and write about the era, the culture and the zeitgeist that was the humble VHS tape, but I think from now on I will have to leave the serious collecting to the people with the serious money.

I'll buy tapes I want and love. I'm thankfully not a completist or the house would have even more VHS tapes in it than it already does, and its current VHS content is already pretty damn high.

VHS ate my brain. It sucked it out of my head, chewed it up and spat it back into my skull in a far more entertaining state, full of monsters and blood and gore and ninjas and ghosts and psychopaths and heroes and scream queens and so much more. It opened a doorway into a world away from my own, and while it would never solve all of my problems, VHS allowed me the headspace to be able to calm down and deal with them better. Escapism. An edge of taboo and danger. A scary yet exhilarating feeling that you didn't know what was going to happen when you popped a tape into you player. No scene selection, no audio commentaries, no frills. Just films. Just tapes. Just dreams and laughter and nightmares and excitement of every variety.

And long may those tapes play on.

    Happy hunting,

    Andrew Hawnt

About the author

Andrew writes for POWERPLAY ROCK AND METAL MAGAZINE, HORRORNEWS.NET, LOST IN THE MULTIPLEX and anyone else who will let him rant about pop culture and films which are laughably bad but which he seems to enjoy for some reason. He spent nine years working in a comic shop and would rather like those nine years back.

Andrew can be found rummaging in charity shops and flea markets for old horror flicks on VHS or dusty sci-fi paperbacks. He is known by friends and family as a bacon and caffeine addict. Andrew lives in Nottingham, UK with his lady and their son, who is far better looking than his daddy. That wouldn't be hard though, as Andrew still claims to look like an angry potato.

Also by Andrew Hawnt:
ACROSS THE SEAS OF MIND
ACCESS NO AREAS
DEAD THING
FOR THE FALLEN
DIARY OF A GENRE ADDICT VOLUME 1
BAGGED AND BOARDED: LIFE ON PLANET GEEK

Coming next:
DIARY OF A GENRE ADDICT VOLUME 2

Printed in Great Britain
by Amazon.co.uk, Ltd.,
Marston Gate.